I0684410

www.thehummingbirdreview.com
Vol. IV   Issue No. 1   Spring/Summer 2013

Ri
PUBLISHING

Published by Ri Publishing, Laguna Woods, CA, USA
www.thehummingbirdreview.com

The Hummingbird Review presents fine writing by both new writers and fully established literary figures. The review is committed to portraying the beauty and challenges of life—the full human experience—through literature and art, and promotes cross-cultural writing in all forms.

Publisher/Executive Editor
Charles Redner

Editor
Robert Yehling

Associate Editors
Thea Iberall
Michael Scofield

Permissions:

"The Man Who Beat Hemingway,"
Martín Espada, by permission of the author.

FOR SPECIAL THANKS
We also like to thank Eliza Fisher of the Steven Barclay Literary Agency for beginning the process that led to the Billy Collins interview; Judy Studebaker, and Professor Whitney Smith at the College of Southern Idaho, for their assistance in developing the Bill Studebaker retrospective; and Martha Halda for her assistance at the Collins interview.

Cover painting by David Milton, *www.davidmiltonstudio.com*
Cover and book design by Terry Houseworth, *www.houseworthdesign.com*

ISBN: 978-0-9855583-38

Printed in the United States of America

The Man Who Beat Hemingway
By Martín Espada

—for Kermit Forbes, Key West, Florida, 1994

In 1937, Robert Johnson
still sang the Walking Blues,
the insistent churchbell of his guitar,
the moaning congregation of his voice,
a year before the strychnine flavored
his whiskey.

In the time of Robert Johnson,
you called yourself Battling Geech,
135 pounds, the ball of your bicep rolling
when you sickled the left hook
from a crouch, elbows blocking
hammers to the ribcage.
Florida for a black man
was Robert Johnson, moaning:
the signs that would not feed you
hand-lettered in diner windows,
the motels that kept all beds white.

Here, in a ring rigged behind the mansion,
next to the first swimming pool
in Key West, you sparred with Hemingway.
He was 260 pounds in 1937, heavy arms
lunging for you, so you slid crablike
beneath him, your shaven head
spotlit with sweat against his chest.
Only once did his leather fist tumble you,
sprawling across canvas
white as sun.

Now, nearing eighty, one eye stolen

from the socket, one gold tooth
anchored to your jaw,
you awoke this morning
and weighed the hurricane-heavy air
of Key West in your fighter's hands,
three decades after Papa Hemingway
choked himself with a shotgun.
You stand before the mansion
on Whitehead Street, telling the amazed tourists
that you are the man who beat Hemingway,
and it happened here,
even if the plaque
leaves out your name.

TABLE OF CONTENTS
Vol. IV, No. 1 • Spring/Summer 2013

CHARLES REDNER

Publisher's Statement
Sing Praise for the Words!

Why a Hollywood theme?

I did not choose the topic; the theme declared itself. It began with a phone call from my cousin, Jamie McCloskey. "Charlie, guess who's sitting on my sofa?" I was silent, so she added a first name: Bobby. No common relative or acquaintance came to mind, so I gave in and asked, "Bobby who?"

"Bobby De Niro!"

I stared at the phone. Why on earth was this famous actor visiting her Philadelphia suburban home? And just how long had it taken for her relationship to progress from Mr. De Niro to Robert to just plain Bobby? My cousin explained that her house had been selected for shooting a scene of *Silver Linings Playbook*, later nominated for a Best Picture Oscar.

Soon after Jamie's call, Bobby, Jennifer Lawrence, Bradley Cooper, and writer-director David O. Russell scurried around her house. Over the next few months, I received daily updates on the film's progress.

This tale now turns a little surreal. A second home selected on the same block for location shoots belonged to a close friend of my old Philly advertising buddy, Michael Gillespie. Then, a week later, I was invited to a Hollywood studio to evaluate a screenplay for—you guessed it— *Silver Linings Playbook*.

Soon after, I posed a question to our *Hummingbird Review* editors: "How do we combine a Hollywood theme with literature?" They jumped on the challenge, and titles for articles rapidly flowed: "History of Hollywood with Literature," "Adapting Literature to Film," and "Evolution of the Screenwriter." The editors also recalled that many screenwriters, actors, and directors have written poetry. I remembered an incident from when I attended drama school that might make for an on-theme personal essay.

1

All we had to do was attach a writer to a title and, *ta-da: "The Hummingbird Review* Meets Hollywood."

In addition, Editor Robert Yehling tracked down U.S. Poet Laureate (2001-2003) Billy Collins for a one-on-one talk. Bob also obtained permission to publish a suite of poems of the late Bill Studebaker, Idaho's Poet Laureate for many years. Thanks also to poet Martín Espada for "The Man Who Beat Hemingway," and Academy Award-winning screenwriter Michael Blake for his poem, "Hollywood."

One of the most influential authors of our time, George Orwell, would not have lived long enough to write *Animal Farm* and *Nineteen Eighty-Four* if my friend's father hadn't saved his life during combat action in the Spanish Civil War. In keeping with the mysteries of this issue's content, David Milton just happened to have a screenplay about his father, Harry Milton. We had to include an excerpt for you. In addition, David graciously provided our cover art. *Muchas gracias, Señor Milton.*

Finally, we have been blessed with works of not one, but two, advisors to the Smithsonian Institution. For poetry, there is the aforementioned Billy Collins, and for contemporary music, Stevie Salas. Stevie, along with John Doe of "X" fame, have provided the poetry of their song lyrics to our impressive lineup.

As is our custom, we have included previously unpublished writers along with established authors. Those new writers add many gems to this special collection of essays, poems, and prose.

Welcome to our Hollywood edition – hope you enjoy the show. "Lights, camera ... and, action!"

Charles Redner, publisher
Laguna Woods, CA
April, 2013

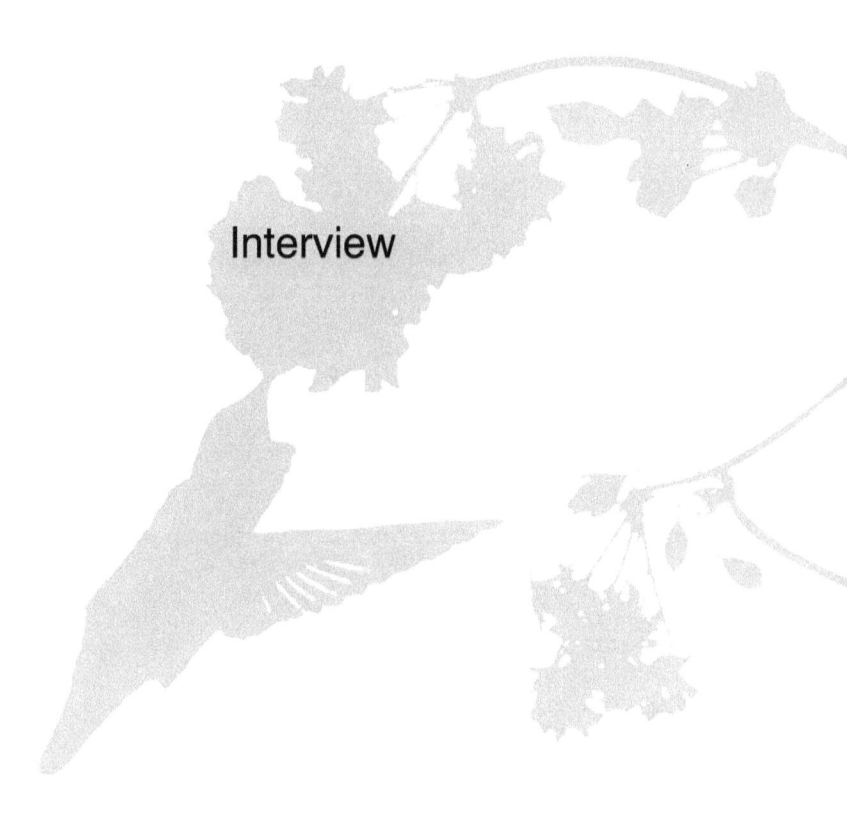

Interview

THE HUMMINGBIRD REVIEW
INTERVIEW: BILLY COLLINS

By Robert Yehling

We've seen more formal poets than Billy Collins. Others have been more critically praised and celebrated. You won't find Billy mentioned often in a discussion about poets who changed the way we think, or revolted against the status quo, or viewed the past, present and future of humankind. Although he would be most capable of writing a hilarious dust-up of these last four lines!

When you step beyond the often humorous ripples in his poems, and the way he can be dead serious one moment and poke fun at poetry itself in another, one fact stands above all else: Billy Collins has done more than anyone else in a half-century to make poetry appealing to the general public. His appearances on NPR's *Fresh Air* and *A Prairie Home Companion* gave him an instant platform. He used his two years as Poet Laureate of the U.S. to create and drive "Poetry 180," one of the most successful approaches ever developed to share poetry in the classroom. And he brushed off the gray skies of many reading atmospheres to inject warmth, wit and hilarity into the night, delighting sell-out crowds along the way.

Quick: name another living poet whose sales top 100,000 copies *per collection*. Now 72, Billy's collections make poetry not only approachable, but also friendly, endearing and rewarding. Whether he deals with serious subjects – such as death, aging, or the difficult side of love – or lighter fare, he finds the common threads in life and teases out their extraordinary jewels. This is why collections like *Sailing Alone Around the Room, The Trouble with Poetry, Taking Off Emily Dickinson's Clothes, The Art of Drowning*, and his two most recent, *Ballistics* and *Horoscopes for the Dead*, are favorites among poetry and non-poetry fans alike. His newest collection, *Aimless Love: New and Selected Poems 2003-2013*, will release in October.

The Hummingbird Review caught up with Billy in late February, when he escaped the cold New York climes for a few days to visit Point Loma Nazarene University in San Diego. He talked with Professor Dean Nelson's students, read to a sell-out crowd, and then joined Dean for a fabulous hour-long, one-on-one conversation that offered equal parts insight, reflection, and humor. Prior to that, we visited with Billy on the water at nearby Shelter Island after he subjected himself to a round of golf on the difficult Torrey Pines South course.

HBR: Are you in San Diego as part of a tour, or is this a one-off?

BC: In and out. My publisher will have me running all over the place in October, when *Aimless Love* comes out.

HBR: So you're here to enjoy this tough midwinter weather (sunny and 65 degrees during the interview).

BC: Yeah, it's tough! I can see why no one wants to leave.

HBR: You had your chance, since you went to graduate school at UC-Riverside.

BC: I guess I did …

HBR: In your recent works, particularly *Ballistics* and *Horoscopes for the Dead*, you spent a lot of time focusing on your mortality. You gave it both serious and comical treatment, but that seems to be the subject. Is this a by-product of growing older, of your aging process?

BC: We're not getting any younger, which is one of the four themes of lyric poetry. It could be a sense of my mortality, but I've had that since I was ten. I remember realizing I was going to die when I was ten years old, and being quite preoccupied if not terrified by it – and entertained by it, in a way. At the same time, kind of fascinated by it.

The message of poetry is, 'Life is great, but you're going to die.' That's basically *carpe diem*. It is, in a sense, a combination of my own mortality, but I'm writing poetry. When I write poetry, I have a sense of being in a tradition. There are themes to be sustained, for good reason, and *carpe diem* is one of them. So I think it's very basic. I tell students, 'If you're majoring in English, you're majoring in death. That's the subject.'

HBR: You've previously said that, were you to run into yourself as a young poet, you wouldn't recognize that person. When asked, you said your poetry has become simpler and more accessible as you've grown older. Could you elaborate?

BC: Sure! When I was a young poet, I was committing all the sins of teenage poets. I was taking myself much too seriously. I hadn't read enough poetry, so I really didn't know what I was doing. I was over-influenced by the Beats, or I was reading school poetry, like William Cullen Bryant, and all these 19th century male poets that seemed completely from another verbal planet (chuckles). Not only did I not have the right influences, but I wasn't being influenced by much at all. Maybe the Beat poets. I just couldn't figure it out. I wasn't allowing humor into my poetry; I thought it was forbidden.

What happened didn't happen until I was in my 30s, when I came under the influence of the right poets, the ones that had a progressive and beneficial influence on my writing. Philip Larkin, Thom Gunn, [Langston] Hughes a little bit, also the California poets like Ron Koertge and Gerald Loughlin. Also people like Ron Padgett, Kenneth Koch, those New York guys, all of which created a kind of playground for ideas, made things a little silly. I seemed to fit right in there.

HBR: You recently edited an anthology, *Bright Wings*, that focuses on bird poetry. You've written several poems using birds as vehicles, but also devices like windows, which seem to be your preferred 'place,' as it were. How do birds, or other devices, work with you?

BC: For poets, birds do one of two things: they sing or fly. Poets want to sing with that kind of full-throated ease, as Keats puts it, and this whole idea of 'Wouldst I could fly like thee', this desire for imaginative freedom that is symbolized by bird flight, and by bird migrations and so forth.

Of course, if you write long enough, these themes or obsessions get revealed. I was never aware of myself as a bird poet ... there are a lot of mice in my poems, too. If you write long enough, you'll see that you're obsessed with berries, or wind ... or something. It becomes a kind of favorite metaphor. One of mine happens to be windows. Maybe I'm the window poet, like Yeats is the swan poet or Frost the woods poet.

HBR: You've drawn quite a large audience with your knack for drawing out extraordinary perceptions and even sacred moments from the most common, everyday events, moods or observations. At the same time, you dial down the complexity of it into readily digestible words and images...

BC: You're going to ask, 'How do you do that?' (laughing)

HBR: We won't make you answer that. You get a pass!

BC: Good ... because I'm not so sure there's an answer there.

HBR: What we will ask is, when did you become consciously aware you could extend poetry to a more expanded audience than just hardcore poetry readers?

BC: It was gradual, and then it was very sudden. In my 30s, I learned how to write in pretty much the way I write now. I think I've developed somewhat, changed somewhat, but basically, I figured out something in my 30s. What I figured out was a tone of voice that I still pretty much use.

In terms of readership, it was very simple: it was NPR. It was 1998, I had a book out called *Picnic, Lightning*. Within a few months, I was on Terri Gross, on *Fresh Air,* and I was on *Prairie Home Companion*. That changed everything. It's an audience of three to four million people – times two. They were the perfect audience – college-educated, middle class, book buying people. In terms of career, and visibility and that, it was NPR.

HBR: Then you were named Poet Laureate of the United States (2001-2003).

BC: That was kind of a booster rocket on this whole thing. All these things oddly fell into place. Believe me, world poetry domination was not my objective here (laughs).

HBR: What specific advantages or opportunities does the platform and honor of being Poet Laureate give you?

BC: If you're Poet Laureate, there you suddenly are – in the Library of Congress. It's not so much being in Washington as a government player or something, but you are an employee and a resident in the Library of Congress. You have the library at your disposal, and you're a well-respected big shot in the library. There are enormous material and human resources at your beck and call, so it's silly not to do anything. Although you're allowed to just do nothing.

HBR: What you did was to create a truly landmark program, Poetry 180, which succeeded in re-introducing the vitality of poetry to classrooms nationwide.

BC: After becoming Poet Laureate, I immediately thought of what an awful time I had in high school, and how being a poet was more a matter of getting beaten up in the parking lot than anything else. If you wanted to get beaten up in the parking lot, announcing you're a poet is a shortcut to that. Also in high school, the poems that were taught were hundreds of years old. I wanted to present poetry that

9

would be cool, because being cool is the objective of high school – and it continues to this day (laughs).

I asked myself, 'What could I do for high schools?' What else: show them some poems! That became the Poetry 180 website. I also wanted to detach it from teaching. So the students either receive a poem a day, or have it read to them during daily classroom announcements, or view a pinned-up poem. Teachers are not supposed to talk about it any further. No analysis. That's the big no-no. Just read it and don't say anything about it. Let the students experience it for themselves.

HBR: The results were overwhelming. I look at the explosion of new literary journals in the past decade, and many – perhaps the majority – have been created by twenty-somethings. They are the right age to have benefitted directly from Poetry 180's early years.

BC: That's a really good point. It actually worked, much to my surprise. When it took off, Random House said, 'Why don't we do an anthology of this?' And we ended up doing a second one. All these teachers said, 'It changed how I teach. It changed my students' whole idea of what poetry was. They like it. They ask, "Where's the poem for the day?"' They remind the teacher, 'Give us one of those poems.'

HBR: So poetry has become cool in high schools.

BC: That's right! Now instead of making fun of you, the mean girls – the beautiful, socially popular girls – want you to read poems to them (laughs).

HBR: Part of your own popularity has to do with the way you view poetry – tongue in cheek, a lot of the time. Within your poems, you commentate about the state of poetry, or how to read poetry, or something about poetry people look for.

BC: I think it all comes out of my being very self-conscious about being a poet. I don't just take it for granted. It's a little embarrassing to me, to be poet, because it's a bit of an absurd thing to be. Just to take that much of an interest in your own speculations, because that's the subject of your poetry. You're not writing about World War II, or a memoir about growing up in a certain environment. You're just writing about ...that tree. Looking at that tree. That's the subject of lyric poetry (chuckles). It's pretty much observational poetry. There's something so egotistical about it, that once in awhile, I feel like I have to write a poem that makes fun of poetry, makes fun of poetry readings ... I have a poem called 'Workshop' that is sort of a parody of a writing workshop. I have a poem called 'Irish Poetry' which is a satire on Seamus Heaney and a certain type of poem. I want to mix it up; I want to have an irreverent attitude toward the whole process. I think I'm trying to balance, or hide, how seriously I take the process, how seriously I take poetry. I just don't want to be caught taking it too seriously. It's probably a defense mechanism in a way ... now that you're dragging it out of me.

HBR: We've noticed this has rubbed off on some of your protégés, most notably spoken word maestro Taylor Mali. Poke fun at the process, deliver poems that look mildly humorous when read silently, but are hilarious when recited – but then hit audiences between the eyes with poems that really make them think, look into themselves.

BC: It should be all of that. The whole phenomenon of poetry is so serious. Go to a poetry reading; people are serious! The whole thing is so gray ... I just like to shoot up the room a little bit. Like my book, *The Trouble with Poetry*. The trouble with poetry is that there's just too much friggin' poetry! I just like saying stuff like that. I'm trying to avoid going down that other road. By "that other road," I mean the sense that poetry is vital, that it's another world, it's another place. It's different from the place we live in. That's why I read poetry; to be transported to this other place, which is a place of the imagination.

HBR: Such as you do with two of your newer poems, "Gold" and "Four Moon Planet". Those are absolute gems. In the latter poem, you epigram Robert Frost and take it from there. What kind of an impact did Frost make on you, since you were in college when he read "The Road Less Traveled" at President Kennedy's Inauguration?

BC: None – at first. I was going with these jokers, these hard-irony poets, not that Frost doesn't have some of that. Guys like James Tate, Ron Padgett, Philip Larkin, who are extremely playful. Don't get me wrong; Frost can be playful, too. However, the things you learn from Frost have to do with craft, how to switch gradually from something very simple to something very expansive and vital. Like walking in the woods, and there's two roads, and suddenly, it's just the TWO ROADS. Everything becomes capitalized in your mind.

He came to my college (Holy Cross) when I was there. By that time, he was ancient. I could have lunch with him, because I was on the literary magazine, but it was a Jesuit college. The message (from faculty) was, 'Don't say anything at lunch, because you'll just make an ass out of yourself, and bring disgrace on the school.' (chuckles)

HBR: That's 'liberating'!

BC (laughing): It's the Jesuits in the '60s, you know? So I never spoke to Frost, but we ate lunch in the same room. We'd just look up at him … occasionally.

But Frost is the master of rhythmic and rhyme poetry. Like Yeats, he is a model of that extremely refined craft. Then there's always something else going on in his poems. That other hidden thing has to be taught, in a way, because young people can't pick it up. The classic example of a misunderstood Frost poem is "Good Fences Make Good Neighbors". All about neighborly camaraderie, right? No; that poem is *against* that epithet. It's written as a criticism of that sentence. He's widely misunderstood, because there are quotes pulled out of his poems and turned into little samplers.

HBR: A poem of yours which goes along those lines is "Brightly Colored Boats Upturned on the Banks of the Charles," which kicks off *Ballistics*. The whole poem seems to be right there – in the title. Was that your plan?

BC: Yeah, that's making fun of poetry. What's there to say that isn't said in the title? Where do I go from here?

HBR: What are your feelings about the titling of poems, the titles we choose? We see so many works, in all genres, where the title either doesn't seem to connect to the work, or it's too obscure.

BC: There are two kinds of titles: the simple title, like "Soap," or "Monday," or "Poolside," a little locator like that; and then titles like "Brightly Colored Boats Upturned on the Banks of the Charles," that are very informational. James Wright had those titles like, "Lying in a Hammock (on William Duffy's Farm in Pine Island) Minnesota," or "In Response to a Rumor that the Last Existing Whorehouse in Wheeling, West Virginia Has Been Condemned." Those are good, because it pushes all that information in the title and you don't have to deal with it in the first stanza. You don't have to bother with the scene and setting stuff.

HBR: What is a title's most important function?

BC: The main thing about titles is this: You shouldn't use, in the title, the information *you have*, as the poet, which the reader doesn't have. Let's say you've written ten drafts of this poem. You put it in your drawer, and you work on it the next week. And the week after. Well, you're so into this damned thing, you know? And then here's this poor reader, who's wandering down the street and bumps into your poem, and you have a title that is something like, "Serpentine Vortex of My Consciousness". Maybe *you* know what that's about! (laughs)

You should never put above a poem a title that only you can under-stand, or that depends upon the benefit of having been inside the poem. It's like insider trading. The title is the way the reader steps into the poem; it should be unobstructed.

HBR: In October 2013, you're coming out with *Aimless Love*, a book of new and collected poetry from the past ten years. Can you give us a little preview?

BC: Well, more "Gold" … I like the fact you like "Gold." That's about the sun coming up …(recites) *When the sun begins to rise/ and reflects off the water/the whole room is suffused with the kind/ of golden light that might travel/at dawn on the summer solstice/the length of a passageway in a megalithic tomb* …

HBR: …And you spend the entire poem comparing the sunrise to famous mythological, historical and literary references to gold, all the while saying you're not going to do that.

BC: And *that's* a very self-conscious poem. If I compare it to this, you wouldn't believe me, and I don't want to push this too far, but then I do it. It's this whole wheel-spinning series of similes that ends with Dante.

HBR: In that case, we'll take more "Gold"!

BC: OK (laughs)! *Aimless Love* is basically ten years of poetry There are about fifty new poems. I've had one new-and-selected be-fore, *Sailing Alone Around the Room*. Usually, there are maybe fif-teen to twenty new poems. They wanted this to be a really big book. For a poetry book, it's going to be immense – about 160 pages. So you're going to get the best of four books, and then fifty new poems.

* * * * *

Billy Collins, a keynote presenter at the February 2013 "Sym-posium by the Sea," Point Loma Nazarene University, sat for a discussion after his reading with the event organizer, Dr. Dean Nelson. Near the end of the talk, Nelson offered up this "Collins-like" poem:

While Preparing To Interview Billy Collins
By Dean Nelson

The stack of books came two, three at a time from Amazon,
Creating an online clamor from other poets
Who said, "People who buy Billy Collins poems also like me
And often buy us together."

But I am monogamous for the time being
And read about details of his life
Where he is swinging from a hammock,
Lighting a cigarette,
Listening to Thelonious Monk, and I wonder

Why my life details seem so dull.
But they are like his details,
Which are profound.

The faint tapping from the crockpot, like a heartbeat
Reminds me that my daughter is coming over
For dinner tonight
So my wife can help her with her taxes.

I walk to the closet to get my vitamins –
Seven each morning
To ward off the deadly sins of heart disease, cancer,
Prostate enlargement, muscle loss, bone loss, the common cold
And all other maladies not yet discovered.

My hand hovers over other jars –
The hemlock, the arsenic, the anthrax,

And I decide to swallow those later
If the interview with Billy goes badly.

Preparing for Billy Collins has me reading poems all of the time
Instead of only when I grieve.

I lie in bed and think about the Big Dipper
Spilling ink into the sky, and taking off Emily Dickinson's clothes,
And a three-year-old reciting *Litany*.
I descend into deep water below Earth's surface,
Past the fracking, into the core,

Where I crawl out of the ooze, amoeba-like,
Then wriggle like a tadpole, grow short legs, then arms
That pull me onto land, then longer legs strong enough to hold me
    upright.
Then I'm running, then flying

Suspended in the updraft of his next stanza,
Where the poetry creates lift
And I can see into the light.

Literature and Hollywood:
Prose

The Marriage of Literature and Hollywood

One morning in 1908, a group of actors and extras joined director J. Stuart Blackton in New York's Central Park to shoot a ten-minute, one-reel silent film. The studio, Vitagraph, had produced hundreds of one-reelers and short subjects for use in the highly popular Nickelodeon viewers. The studio chief, Thomas Edison, invented the light bulb, masterminded the use of electricity, and owned the first movie studio in the United States.

This new film, *Romeo & Juliet*, ventured into virginal cinematic territory for U.S. flickers: combining literature with moving pictures. Six years prior, Georges Melies had adapted Jules Verne's 1865 sci-fi novel *From the Earth to the Moon* into *La Voyage dans la Lune (A Trip to the Moon)*, five minutes that brought special effects and scenario-writing into the new medium. Now, in New York, Edison and Blackton presented a film starring Paul Panzer and Florence Lawrence. Lawrence would go on to sign with D.W. Griffith's Biograph Studios and become the Biograph Girl, then the world's first credited star. *Romeo & Juliet* broke down the floodgates, opening up the rich content of plays, novels and biographies for future scenarios (screenplays).

A century later, we consider the marriage of literature and film second nature. Shakespeare's work has been the most filmed, with more than 250 pictures to date between 23 adapted plays. There have been 82 versions of *Hamlet* (61 motion pictures, 21 TV movies). Another 40 versions of *Romeo & Juliet* have been filmed; a new iteration premiered in February 2013, starring Damian Lewis and Hailee Steinfeld.

Countless thousands of motion pictures have been adapted from literary works, bringing to the big screen characters, plots and settings once envisioned solely in our minds: the romantic and scenic sweep of D.H. Lawrence's *Lawrence of Arabia*, Margaret Mitchell's *Gone with the Wind* and Boris Pasternak's *Doctor Zhivago*; the hubris of John Steinbeck's *Grapes of Wrath*; the soul-wrenching dilemmas in Herman Melville's *Moby Dick* and Ernest Hemingway's *Old Man and the Sea*; dramatic pre-Revolutionary War adventure in James

Fenimore Cooper's *The Last of the Mohicans*; the legal tension of Harper Lee's *To Kill a Mockingbird*; the human cost of the Civil War in Charles Frazier's *Cold Mountain* and Stephen Crane's *Red Badge of Courage*; the exotic romance of Henry James' *Wings of the Dove*; and films based on much more recent literary treasures, such as Sue Monk Kidd's *The Secret Life of Bees*, Frances Mayes' *Under the Tuscan Sun* and Audrey Niffenegger's *The Time Traveller's Wife*.

We could name thousands of others. We all have our favorites. What is lesser known is that thousands of poems have also been written about movie stars, movies and specific characters by the likes of Allen Ginsberg, Denise Levertov, Sharon Olds, Jack Kerouac, Wanda Coleman, David Meltzer, Maya Angelou, John Ashbery, John Updike and countless others – including *Dances With Wolves* author Michael Blake, whose poem "Hollywood" appears in this issue.

Now, *The Hummingbird Review* casts its hat into the ring. Much of this issue is devoted to the relationship between literature and film. Enjoy.

ADAM RODMAN

Adapting Literature to Film

One of the most daunting tasks for any screenwriter is to take someone else's work, whether a poem, short story, play, novel, or true-life story, and reshape it into a screenplay. Before the work even begins, questions arise: What obligations do you owe to the original material? Can you change the details of a person's life to suit your dramatic needs? Is it right to take a novel that you love, and change it to fit your vision? Is that fair to the novel's readers? Can you combine events and characters in order to make the screenplay work better?

The first time I grappled with these daunting problems occurred when I was a student at the American Film Institute, and tasked with writing a 30-minute screenplay adaptation. I decided to adapt Irwin Shaw's short story, "Whispers in Bedlam". The resulting script was a complete disaster: true to the story almost word-for-word, way too long, and deeply boring.

I couldn't understand what had gone so wrong. My patient instructors tried to walk me through the difference between a movie script and a short story. "But – but – that's Irwin Shaw. I can't change his words. That's some of the best prose in the English language," I objected. I believed that changing a word would be an affront to Shaw and to writers everywhere. My instructors explained (some in a kindly tone, others more firmly) that "Whispers in Bedlam" would be just fine with or without my help. People still could buy a collection of Shaw's stories, read the one in question, and no adaptation could harm the underlying material. As a screenwriter, my obligation was to the screenplay I was writing and to the resulting movie. To my discredit, I assumed that the instructors had drunk the entertainment industry Kool-Aid, and that I would be the one to bring respect back to novelists and short story writers everywhere.

All I can say in my defense is that I was twenty years old. So I knew everything! By the time I was about to graduate from film school, I not only had begun to think about my instructors' advice, but also internalized some of the principles in a way that worked for me.

As part of a graduate project, I wrote an adaptation of William Styron's brilliant novel, *Sophie's Choice*. I edited that fine, lengthy work down to about 45 minutes. If I had been a little less loyal to the underlying material, I may have whittled it to a lightning quick 30 minutes or so – and better for that fact.

In adapting *Sophie's Choice,* the key was to determine what moved me about the story. I tried to recreate that feeling in the screenplay, with movie pacing and cinematic conventions such as only including narratively relevant scenes, and reducing dialogue to its barest and most essential elements. I had begun to form a philosophy of adaptation: the job of the screenwriter is to translate the underlying truth of the novel into the visual language of film.

Aside from literary morality, I also grappled with how to pick and choose the facts of a real-life story in order to arrive at a satisfactory fictional tale. I had been working on a fictional story about a young South African man who comes to America. In my screenplay, he was an only child. This began to bother me. Large families were the norm in South Africa. Why would my character be an only child? Because I wanted it that way? Because it was useful for my story? Unsatisfied with the answers, I added three brothers and sisters, then six, then even more. Now I had something closer to the truth, but it made the script a mess. I was stuck between reality and a hard place. The idea that I was somehow cheating reality bothered me more and more, until finally I solved the problem by writing a scene in which my character's mother explains that she is no longer capable of bearing children. "I'm broken that way," she tells her son. As a result of that scene, we begin to understand why she and her husband are so protective of their son.

The lesson: while reality is important, there are always conflicting truths. If you can't use the most obvious set of facts, then find others. Choose the facts that are most useful to your story. Truth be told, the lesson I should have drawn from this experience was *never* to let reality interfere with dramatization.

My philosophy about literary adaptations encountered a powerful challenge in the form of my first professional feature film assignment, an adaptation of *The Serpent and the Rainbow,* a non-fiction book by Wade Davis. I found myself contemplating many chapters about the history of poison, Haitian history, and voodoo culture – a buffet of fascinating stuff. I wanted to do right by Wade Davis, a Harvard ethnobotanist. Though I chose to take certain fictional liberties, I aimed to maintain the realistic tone of the book. When the executive producer suggested particular changes that would make the piece more dramatic, I refused. "That didn't happen," I told him. "Nothing like that happened!" I may have been right about the facts, but I was wrong about the drama.

Like many educational experiences in life, the learning curve of screenwriting seems to move one step forward and two steps back. I was hired by Universal to adapt a former DEA agent's life story. Yet again, I wanted to stick as close to the real story as possible. The actual incidents took place in the 1970s, so I wanted to set my story in the 1970s. I wanted to keep all the details the same. Seeing a pattern here? The producers were supportive of me and agreed to argue the case with the studio, but the studio insisted that the story be told in the present. Whether it was my gratitude for the offer of support that made me want to help out my producers, or a little commercial soul-searching, I cannot recall, but I came up with a way to tell the story in a contemporary time frame. I changed everything, keeping only the barest thematic underpinnings of the man's life. The resulting script was great. Everyone thought I did a terrific job. Even the former DEA agent loved it. I was on my way to getting the hang of this adaptation stuff.

Or so I thought.

The next adaptation to come my way was a science fiction classic, *Bug Jack Barron,* by Norman Spinrad. I love science fiction, and *Bug Jack Barron* is a seminal piece. The director attached to the project was Costa-Gavras, whose work I greatly admire. What could go wrong? It was Irwin Shaw all over again: I remained faithful to the novel to a fault, and did a disservice to Norman Spinrad, Costa-Gavras, and myself.

While licking my wounds from *Bug Jack Barron*, I grew more and more certain I would never attempt an adaptation again.

Then I received a movie-of-the-week assignment about an incident in Bensonhurst, New York: a young black man had been murdered by a white teenager, who mistakenly thought the victim had been dating his girlfriend and had caused her to break up with him. The murder triggered terrible riots, exposing an underlying racial animus that threatened to tear the city apart. The producers, terrifically supportive, gave me the freedom to handle the fictional version of events in any way I thought best. Gulp.

I interviewed as many people as possible about the event. I wandered the streets of Bensonhurst, Crown Heights, and other areas of Brooklyn affected by the violence. After agonizing for a few weeks, I made the decision to create an entirely fictional version of the actual events. Thus liberated, I turned in a script that fortuitously synthesized lessons that I had absorbed from my earlier efforts, to look for both the underlying truths in the incident and in the citywide reactions. In allowing myself the freedom to invent completely fictional dramatic through-lines, I served the story and depicted the core reality of the truth, as best I could interpret it.

Some thirty years after my run-in with Irwin Shaw, I have come to the following conclusion: it is never easy to adapt something. I ultimately believe that the writer's loyalty must lie with the screenplay. This belief will be severely tested with each adaptation. Beginning with my newest project. Recently, I was hired to adapt a true-life story that took place during the Holocaust. If ever a situation demanded veracity and tested the bounds of dramatic morality, surely this era and its events would comprise that circumstance.

Did I mention adaptations are difficult?

MANNY PACHECO

Evolution of the Screenwriter

It seems no novel has been adapted to the screen more than *The Great Gatsby*. F. Scott Fitzgerald's work has been filmed five times, and once again is in production. Notable versions include a 1926 silent film starring Warner Baxter and a very young William Powell; a 1949 Golden Age motion picture with Alan Ladd and Shelly Winters; and arguably, the most popular adaptation in 1974, featuring Robert Redford, Mia Farrow, Bruce Dern and Sam Waterston, and a script by Francis Ford Coppola. The upcoming epic will star Leonardo DiCaprio, Carey Mulligan, and Tobey Maguire.

Fitzgerald joined Ernest Hemingway as American authors of novels and short stories, whose works reflected the times known as the *Jazz Age*. Before the start of their significant careers, though, literature of noted living scribes was not considered viable material for the stage and screen. Of course, early scenario writers often adapted the great works of Shakespeare, Dickens, Victor Hugo, Robert Louis Stevenson, and Jack London. And, science fiction translated well on the silent screen (especially H.G. Wells and Jules Verne, whose 1865 novel *From the Earth to the Moon* became *La Voyage das la Lune [A Trip to the Moon]*, Georges Melies' 1902 classic and the first film to use special effects).

Influenced by the very-real social commentary of Sinclair Lewis and Upton Sinclair, Fitzgerald and Hemingway used actual history as a backdrop to their fictional stories. Gertrude Stein dubbed these survivors of World War I (The Great War) as the *Lost Generation*, which included composer Cole Porter, singer Josephine Baker, dancer Isadora Duncan, and painter Pablo Picasso, among others. John Steinbeck also comes to mind as an American author who developed fiction based on the normal, if dreary, lives of real people. It was T.S. Eliot who first popularized the notion of turning modern fiction into dramatic theatre. Recently, Woody Allen paid homage to these artists of the *Lost Generation* in his 2012 film, *Midnight in Paris*.

Eugene O'Neill introduced stylistic realism into American drama, associated with the work of Russian playwright Anton Chekhov, Norwegian writer Henrik Ibsen, and Swedish playwright August Strindberg. American theatre was forever changed. Billed as an alternative to the light musical comedy revues from folks like Florenz Ziegfeld, O'Neill's plays captured the imagination of a nation by including dialogue in a popular vernacular. They involved characters on the fringes of society who struggle to maintain their hopes and aspirations, but ultimately slide into disillusionment and despair. These plots resonated with Depression-era audiences.

This style of writing led to the development of Broadway thespians, eventually discovered by movie moguls searching for new stars for their *talkies* of the 1930s. Actors such as Spencer Tracy, James Cagney, Paul Muni, Gary Cooper, Clark Gable, and Humphrey Bogart emerged in realistic cinematic dramas based on the writings of Hemingway, Steinbeck, and O'Neill. Early entries popular among filmgoers included *A Farewell to Arms, Strange Interludes,* and *Of Mice and Men.*

In the thirties, a European style of filmmaking became popular as Axis aggression swept two continents. Writers such as Dashiell Hammett and Raymond Chandler were quickly hired by the movie studios to update how gangster-films were put together. The resulting genre became known as *film noir.* Hammett was particularly adept at this gritty nuanced style, since elements of the technique were introduced in the *Thin Man* series of motion pictures of the 1930s. It came together with the 1941 production of *The Maltese Falcon.* The underlying theme, of a hero with duplicitous motives who menaced dark evening streets and met up with a *femme fatale*, made stars of Alan Ladd, John Garfield, Veronica Lake, Robert Mitchum, William Bendix and others. Iconic movies, including *The Glass Key, Out of the Fog, Double Indemnity, The Postman Always Rings Twice,* and *The Asphalt Jungle*, still play remarkably well in rich black-and-white cinematography, and a fascinating *film noir* script.

Meanwhile, new productions were developed from Hemingway, Steinbeck, and O'Neill. *For Whom the Bell Tolls, The Grapes of Wrath, Tortilla Flat,* and *Mourning Becomes Electra* were among the many works receiving accolades from the Academy of Motion Picture Arts and Sciences each year. These fine motion pictures inspired a new generation of author/playwrights. Tennessee Williams and Arthur Miller began influencing how actors studied their craft.

The Lee Strasberg Theatre and Film Institute trained actors in a technique known as *The Method*. This teaching style owed much to the Russian director, Stanislavsky, whose book, *An Actor Prepares*, dealt with the psychology of interpretive acting. Actors such as Marlon Brando, James Dean, Paul Newman, Montgomery Clift, and Marilyn Monroe, and directors like Elia Kazan and Sidney Lumet, embraced this theatrical concept.

This acting technique was extraordinarily popular in live television of the 1950s, particularly in anthology dramas of the day. Teleplay writers emerged; the works of Rod Serling and three-time Academy Award-winning screenwriter Paddy Chayevsky come to mind. Rod Steiger, Robert Redford, Lee Remick, Joanne Woodward, George C. Scott, Jack Klugman, and Cloris Leachman, among others, were plucked from the small screen to become cinematic stars. *Requiem for a Heavyweight, Patterns,* and *Twelve Angry Men* were adapted into successful film productions.

Later, Dustin Hoffman, Robert De Niro, Al Pacino, Harvey Keitel ushered in a new-realism that exists in movies today. The Hays Code, established in the 1930s, was the first casualty of this modern-day cinematic revolution. The Motion Picture Ratings were created in 1967 to help families decide which films might be appropriate for their children. Screenwriters now had the dramatic license to tackle the most delicate of issues.

It remains to be seen if F. Scott Fitzgerald's work still excites theatregoers. My guess is, if the material is strong and well-adapted, and if the actors hit their marks, then ticket sales will be brisk. *The Great Gatsby* is set for a May 10, 2013 release.

CHARLES REDNER

Let's Play Celebrity

With classes concluded, five students walked outside and down the darkened steps of the Bessie V. Hicks School of Dramatic Arts. It had been a long, long day and night. Now at quarter past ten, they were tired, hungry and looking for a quick bite to eat before heading home.

The renowned drama school, located next to the Betsy Ross House in the Olde City district of Philadelphia, boasts a long history of turning out thespians for Broadway and Hollywood. Its graduates include Jeanette MacDonald and Charles Bronson.

One student yells, "Let's play celebrity!" Four broad smiles emerge, a clear indication of "game-on." The first order of business: draw straws to determine who will be the "celebrity." A tall, slender student, Bruce, wins. He finds a suitable cheap dining establishment and enters the restaurant alone. After a ten-minute wait, the others enter together and select a booth, near Bruce but outside his hearing range.

While Bruce bites into a burger, the others survey their menus as the waitress awaits the orders. One student looks over at Bruce and nudges his booth mate. He whispers, "Hey! Isn't that, oh, I forget his name. He was in that latest John Wayne flick." The students notice the waitress glance over toward Bruce as she walks away with their orders.

Shortly thereafter, a cook peeks from behind the counter at Bruce. A second waitress looks over the cook's shoulder. As the first waitress returns with the meals, the four students are in a hushed, heated discussion as to the correct identity of the "celebrity." Diners in the entire restaurant begin buzzing about the "celebrity" in the room. Having accomplished their job, the foursome eats while Bruce feigns annoyance, lowers his head and pretends to be unaware of the commotion. The joke is on the restaurant employees and guests, who believe Bruce a real celebrity.

But was it a joke at all – or perhaps a rehearsal?

Hummingbird Review

As the years passed, tall, slender Bruce would appear in 142 titles for television and movies. He became the most hated actor in the country for "killing" John Wayne in *The Cowboys*, only to be nominated for the Academy Awards' Best Supporting Actor in *Coming Home*. Bruce played Tom Buchanan brilliantly in the 1974 version of *The Great Gatsby*, and some critics suggested that it would have been a better movie had he been cast as Jay Gatsby instead of Robert Redford. Today, Bruce pops up in television shows like *CSI* and the popular HBO series, *Big Love*, in which he plays Frank Harlow, a major recurring role during the show's six seasons.

Bruce might have become famous without any credits. He was once married to Alan Ladd's daughter and became the father of a *Jurassic Park* star, first name Laura. The student who starred in the early game of celebrity was none other than Bruce Dern.

In 2007, Bruce coauthored his biography appropriately titled, *Things I've Said, But Probably Shouldn't Have:* An Unrepentant Memoir. In the book, Bruce mentions training at the Bessie V. Hicks School of Dramatic Arts, but doesn't confess to pretending to be a celebrity while still learning his craft.

Literature & Hollywood:
Poetry

MICHAEL BLAKE

Hollywood

Hollywood
Is a place where
Faces drop
Backs turn
Doors shut
Tables clear
Phones click off
And voices fall suddenly over cliffs
At the sound of a single word
Even when it's someone's first name
You have to be careful
'Cause if you say that single word
Even by accident
Your dream deal might go
Up in smoke
The word of course is ... *art*.

THEA IBERALL

Me and Meryl Streep

I learned an important lesson from Meryl Streep.
She and I were having breakfast at Izzy's Deli on 15th Street
in Santa Monica. Well, she was sitting at the table
next to me with her two children, two tiny Meryl Streep replicas
with their blonde heads and Meryl Streep noses.
The whole room watched as if she weren't there.
She knew all eyes were on her, but the cocoon surrounding
her and her little cubs said 'mind your own business,
we are normal people eating pancakes with blueberries.'

So I'm walking down Indian Canyon Road in Palm Springs
with my girlfriend, her hand in mine. An arts and crafts street
fair blocks off the cars. Hundreds of people stroll among
patchouli candles, plumeria smells, African lilies and key lime
pie. The sky glints off tables of iron ladies and laser cut tiles.

My girlfriend leans into me and says, "they're all staring at us."
Her red hair swirls in the Mojave light, her pink blouse silks
across her shoulders like a devil in prada. I'm wearing
my baseball cap backwards thinking how well my left hand
fits into her right one. Silver studs mark squares along
my black leather belt, tourists surveying our momma mias
as if we're cockroaches primed on our every move, how our
fingers entwine like wild rivers, how my digit tips study the
microscopic bridges of her distal skin. We're in the middle
of the street. Traffic lights line up like piled postcards, greens

outnumbering the yellows and reds. Behind them
the San Jacinto mountains brush the hours against the late
afternoon sun and the wind dances into a deep ringing. I look into
her eyes, infinite prairies of shy irises and say –
 let me tell you about my breakfast with Meryl Streep.

Thea Iberall
May 2005

RYKA AOKI

From *Sometimes Too Hot the Eye of Heaven Shines*

Someone asks if Hollywood shines at night.
I say Hollywood shines brightest afterhours,
when an underage skirt makes the sidewalk
speak in tongues.

When a bacon-wrapped hot dog spits
at the streetsweeper with a Sunday School voice.
When a needle jabs Sh'ma Yisroel
into a queer punk tweeker's neck
while his father faps to BarebackTwinks.com
a thousand shivas away.

Someone dreams of rain,
of reservoirs feathered with dead gulls and salt.
Of sinkholes, highway cones,
four cars spinning, one upside down.

Someone dreams of genius
slamming flash flood triolets
upon a march of ivory palisades.
I ask God for a filthy toilet.
behind two panes of bulletproof,
the station man glares
not giving a sit or shit what King Lear said …

Soaking in Shakespeare, how sharper
than a serpent's tooth is a child waiting
for the gift of magic words!

KATE HARDING

Gourd Song
(written as Penny Perry)

Gourds covered my mother's garden.
Thin necked, big bellied
with leaves the size of hands,
they crowded Canterbury Bells
that worked so hard to live
under the murderous sun.

"Interloper." My mother,
a New Yorker,
(in love with Wordsworth)
hated L.A. She yanked gourds
by their fleshy stems.
"No English poet ever wrote
an ode to gourds."

"Mexicans make things out of them.
Even musical instruments,"
said my mother's best friend, Dorothy,
Costello to her Abbott,
two hundred pounds in shorts.
My mother stood upright as bamboo.
Their straw hats nodded like sunflowers.

Later, Dorothy painted the gourds
Frida Kahlo blue. Mother strung
them above the hollyhocks.
Shaken by wind, seeds sung
inside the hollowed fruit.
Gourds swayed
as Frida's colorful dresses
once did against the New York skyline.

KATE HARDING

At night my father dreamed
of his lover.
My mother in a peasant dress,
bare feet warmed by patio stones
sipped tequila under the city moon.

CHARLES REDNER

Vampires, Be Gone!

May I have the pleasure?
May I have the pleasure of killing the last vampire,
or will the horrid hordes slay me first?

When I am King, all in the realm will carry, at hand,
freshly bottled Holy Water, mallet with wooden stake,
and a Pope-blessed crucifix.

When I am King, Buffy and True Blood will be banished,
along with novels coddling blood-sucking bats.
The sun will never set at Twilight.

When I am King, statues of Bram Stoker will be smashed.
bios of Bela Lugosi and Lon Chaney stricken from Wikipedia.
Agents, editors and publishers of the genre
may be Tasered on sight.

May I have the pleasure
of murdering them all, or like the gladiators of Rome,
I ask, let me die honorably in the attempt.

GAIL BORNFIELD

Rebirth of a Star

With a sense of familiarity
and a faint recognition, she
reaches back to touch
one last time the life
that once was hers. She pauses,
a smile crossing her lips
as she experiences a sense of
completeness and finality.

Standing on the precipice, she
turns to the present, her thoughts
transformed. Her heart opens.
She is called forward
to experience life with a
deeper understanding and wisdom,
heretofore unknown. Her lens to the
world has been replaced through a
rebirth of the soul.

ROBERT YEHLING

The Price You Pay for Being a Film Addict

(Or, Thoughts After Watching 100 Movies
in the Winter of 2012-13)

I always wonder what will happen
after the lead characters have resolved
their conflicts, or made love,
or died, or turned in opposite directions
to new lives beyond the final frame.

You would think the movie itself
was enough, the months of hard work
laid down by a producer, director,
lead and character actors, cinematographers,
crews, assistants, costume designers & make-up artists.

You would think
I would be satisfied with the director's cut
after screenwriters tried to fashion
the latest great novel or play
into two hours of cinematic pleasure,
their meticulous well-woven jewel
handed to those who will
speak the dialogue and emote the feelings
that made those novels great.
I hope they get it right.

You would think I would fall asleep
thrilled that when *The Time Traveler's Wife*
rode in with *Great Expectations*
to catch her *Wings of a Dove* gondola
after vacationing *Under a Tuscan Sun*,
she was *Gone with the Wind*,

ROBERT YEHLING

reprising with her *Quiet Man*
a *Romeo and Juliet* tradition
that began with a
Central Park one-reeler in 1908 –
or was it 1597, on a creaky wooden stage? –
and came back to cinematic life in 2013

Where I sit now,
remembering why I hate it
when the best movies end,
when characters I've grown to love
fade to credits:

Because I like to turn the page
and keep their stories alive.

ROXANNE PILAT

Sibling Rivalry

The list tells all:
Three hundred and fourteen
other tales mirror the fall down a stairwell.
In wide-screen, black-and-white, or Technicolor,
you can see them. The spindles are loose, or grabbed,
or collapsed under the weight of a body pushed.
The one I remember is of Jane's sister, Blanche,
who never falls, but captive in her wheelchair,
always fears she will.
Looking from the threshold of her bedroom door
Reflecting on the marble-floored foyer below,
Blanche worries that someday one lathed and lacquered rod
will break under her grasp, should she be pushed,
and she will tumble down down past the sixteen risers
all arms all legs all whirligig:
unable to stop the tile rising up up all too fast.
She would end up crippled.
No, she would end up dead.
She is already crippled, Jane reminds her.
And thus corrected, by her tart-tongued nemesis,
She steels her gaze sharp as Anteros' arrow,
at sweet baby Jane, Daddy's favorite,
and grips the handles of the wheeled chair tighter,
as she waits and watches, watches and waits.
"It's my turn to be waited on,"
a duty-full Jane must be thinking,
sensing her sister's gaze,
looking (with Bette Davis eyes)
down the long flight of stairs.

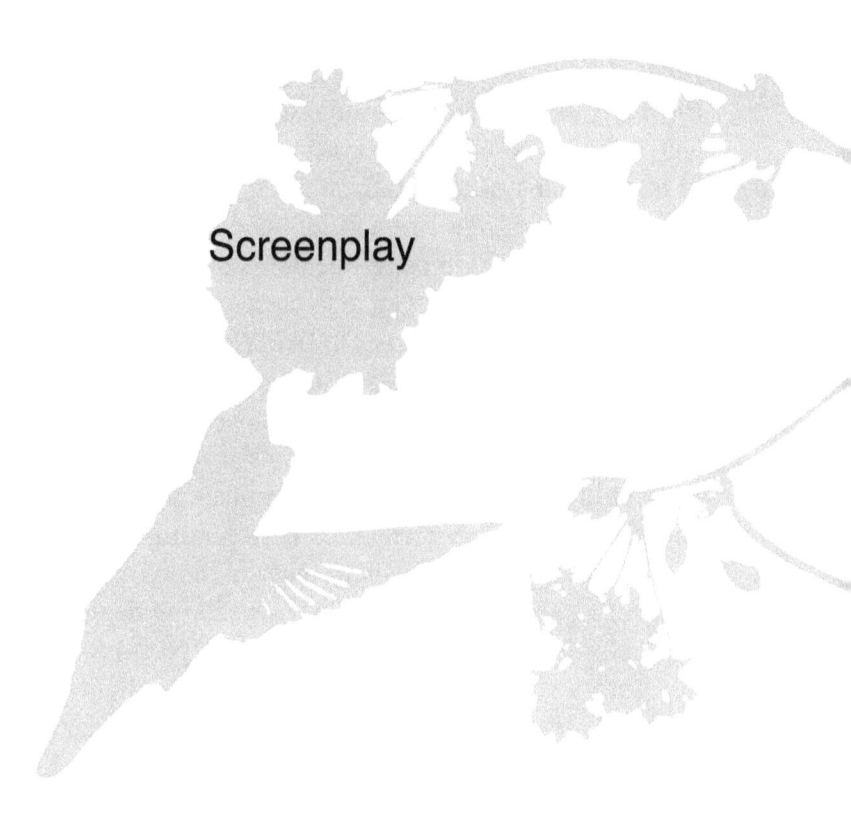

Screenplay

Bayonets and Blood

By Ret Talbot and David Milton

Bayonets and Blood is the untold story of Harry Milton (aka Wolf Kupinsky), who risked everything to fight for fairness and equality in the trenches of the Spanish Civil War and who, in the process, ended up saving the life and influencing the politics of one of the twentieth century's most influential writers. George Orwell, author of *Animal Farm* and *1984*, also elected to join the fight against fascism in Spain in 1936, but, unlike Wolf, Orwell was woefully unaware of the complexity and treacherousness of the political alliances forged and fractured in what became a proxy war between Stalin and Hitler. As Wolf attempts to overcome the odds on the battlefield and prove to himself that one man can make a difference, an unlikely friendship emerges between him and Orwell, and it is that friendship that ultimately may be the only thing that can keep either man alive. While *Bayonets and Blood* deals with politics and a war almost unknown to a contemporary North American audience, it is a story with a remarkable number of parallels to the geopolitics of the twenty-first century. It is also a story that is extremely close to co-author David Milton, who is the son of Harry Milton. *Bayonets and Blood* is Milton's and Talbot's first screenplay and is appearing here for the first time.

FADE IN:

INT. MOTEL - DAY

SUPER: Palo Alto, California. 1980

WOLF KUPINSKY (aka Harry Milton), a short, powerful man in his 70s, opens a file revealing letters and newspaper clippings. Black & white photographs show Trotsky and two dogs, young Wolf in a WWII U.S. Army uniform and a group of men posed by a machine gun with the words "SPAIN, 1937" written at the bottom. MARGOT appears.

> MARGOT
> Pop? You almost ready?

> WOLF
> You've seen this picture, right?

> MARGOT
> Sure, Pop. That's the one with
> George Orwell at the front.

> WOLF
> I hate to give it away.

> MARGOT
> You're not. It's going in the
> archives. Now come on. We're late.

EXT. STANFORD UNIVERSITY - DAY

SUPER: STANFORD UNIVERSITY

Margot steers an old VW bug through the campus gate. A radio story about the Afghan war clashes with the peaceful grounds.

                    NEWSCASTER (O.S.)
                    Today in Afghanistan, violent
                    demonstrations against the Soviet
                    presence again broke out in Kabul.
                    The demonstrators, mostly students,
                    were quickly silenced by Afghan
                    armed forces, communist militia and
                    Soviet troops. The Soviets continue
                    to assume more direct control of
                    the security situation from the
                    Afghan Army, with a series of
                    Soviet offensives against
                    insurgents being reported.

Margot parks the car. A sign reads: HOOVER INSTITUTE AT
STANFORD UNIVERSITY. She gets out and walks around to the
passenger side to help her father. PETER STANSKY greets them.

                    PETER
                    Mr. Milton? I'm Peter Stansky.

                    WOLF
                    The fellow writing the Orwell book?

                    PETER
                    That's correct, Sir. It's a
                    pleasure. Please come in. Bill is
                    waiting for us inside.

INT. HOOVER INSTITUTE ARCHIVES - LATER

BILL ABRAHAMS stands and extends his hand to Wolf.

                    BILL
                    Mr. Milton. I'm Bill Abrahams. It's
                    a pleasure to meet you finally.

Bill gestures to a chair. They all sit. A draft of Orwell,
the Transformation is on the table.

                    PETER
                    This is quite a treat for us. We've
                    met people who knew Orwell, but, to
                    the best of our knowledge, you're
                    the only one who saved his life.
                    Wolf smiles and pulls out the
                    picture of his militia unit.

                    WOLF
                    I knew him as Eric Blair, the
                    soldier. Not George Orwell, the
                    author of Animal Farm and 1984. I'm
                    not sure I saved his life, but I
                    think I taught him a thing or two
                    about politics.

                    PETER
                    Would you mind, Mr. Milton, telling
                    us about the day Orwell was shot?

                    WOLF
                    Nobody in Spain knew me as Harry
                    Milton. There I was Wolf Kupinsky.

                    PETER
                    Was that an alias?

                    WOLF
                    It wasn't legal for Americans to
                    fight for Spain, so I used the name
                    I had started using back in New
                    York to shield my family from my
                    political involvement. It was a

nasty time, you know.

                    BILL
This is a nasty time too.

                    WOLF
I won't disagree with you there.
Anyway, it was May when Eric...I
mean Orwell was shot. 1937. The
Spanish Aragon. The air was
ambrosia; it was like wine...

Wolf sits back in his chair and closes his eyes.

EXT. HUESCA FRONT, SPAIN - DAWN

Silence. The stony red desert lightens, revealing a
battlefield. Two opposing trenches separated by the remnants
of a cherry orchard. A rat scurries. Tin cans litter the
ground. There is coiled barbed wire. Muddy craters and burntout
tree trunks dominate, yet there is subtle beauty too.
Cherries whiten on the few live trees. Small flowers emerge.

EXT. POUM MILITIA TRENCH - CONTINUOUS

Young militiamen exit dugouts. Their dirty uniforms don't
match. Weapons are antiquated. A number are English. A
militiaman pisses beside another who is shaving with red
wine, which is more plentiful on the front than potable
water. Young Wolf relieves ERIC BLAIR (aka GEORGE OR-
WELL).

                    WOLF (V.O.)
Eric was relieving me. Nothing had
happened for days.

EXT. FASCIST TRENCH - MOMENTS LATER

A SNIPER steadies his rifle, peering into the scope. He is a
better equipped, professional soldier. It is difficult to
focus in the flat light. The sun crests a distant hill,
momentarily blinding the Sniper.

EXT. POUM MILITIA TRENCH - CONTINUOUS

>   WOLF (V.O.)
>   We were talking about Barcelona.
>   The May Day fighting in the
>   streets. The Stalinist pigs were
>   closing in, and we knew we weren't
>   safe--neither on the front nor in
>   the rear. Eric was so damn tall and
>   he kept shifting about as we
>   talked. Nothing had happened for so
>   long that we'd all become careless.

EXT. FASCIST TRENCH - CONTINUOUS

Through his scope, the sniper sees Eric's head above the
sandbags. He takes a breath and slowly squeezes the trigger.

EXT. POUM TRENCH - CONTINUOUS

The CRACK of a rifle. Eric collapses. Militiamen crowd in,
including RAMON, a handsome Spaniard in his late twenties.

>   WOLF
>   Are you hit?

>   RAMON
>   Lift him up!
Younger Spanish militiamen, just boys, unleash a barrage of

51

fire. WILLIAMS, an Englishman, crouches down beside Ramon.

                    WILLIAMS
          Get his shirt open!

Williams looks over his shoulder at the boys firing.

                    WILLIAMS (CONT'D)
          Quit firing! Save the ammunition
          for a bloody fascist you can hit.

                    RAMON
          Pare disparar!

                    WOLF
          Give me a knife! Quick.

Eric tries to speak. Blood comes from his mouth. Ramon hands
Wolf a bayonet. Wolf cuts Eric's clothing open exposing a
neck wound. Wolf lifts Eric's head. Blood pools in the soil.
Wolf applies pressure. HARRY, an English medic, arrives.

                    HARRY
          Keep the pressure on, Wolf!

                    ERIC
          (barely audible)
          Where am I hit?

                    WOLF
          The throat.

                    HARRY
          Okay. Let's lift him.

Wolf and Ramon lift Eric. Harry splashes both sides of the

wound with alcohol and applies a field dressing.

                    ERIC
            I'm done. Tell Elaine I love her.

Eric's eyes close. He is placed on a stretcher and carried
down the trench. Sporadic gunfire continues.

EXT. GARMENT DISTRICT, NEW YORK CITY - DAY

SUPER: New York City Garment District, The Previous Summer

INT. GARMENT FACTORY - CONTINUOUS

The sound of machine pistons replaces the sound of gunfire.
Wolf operates a cutting machine. A whistle blows. Wolf checks
his watch, turns off his machine and heads for the door.

EXT. GARMENT DISTRICT STREET - CONTINUOUS

A young Jewish FACTORY WORKER catches up to Wolf.

                    FACTORY WORKER
                Your speech last night was
                inspiring, Wolf. A real call to
                action. I wanted you to know I'll
                be at the protest tomorrow.

                    WOLF
                Good. We can't let Macy's get away
                with supporting Nazi pigs.

                    FACTORY WORKER
                Can we really stop them?
They reach a bus stop. Wolf drops a few coins

in a panhandler's tin and then faces the
factory worker.

                    WOLF
          That depends on our will to act.

                    FACTORY WORKER
          But can our actions really be
          enough? Macy's is a huge company.

                    WOLF
          That kind of thinking, my friend,
          is the capitalist puppeteers' ace
          in the hole. They want you to feel
          powerless. That's why we must act.
A bus stops. Wolf steps onto the bus.

                    WOLF (CONT'D)
          See you tomorrow.

INT. THE MILITANT OFFICE, NYC - LATER

Wolf enters the offices of The Militant, a socialist paper,
abuzz with staff on deadline. ALBERTO, a young Spaniard
sitting at a desk near the door, looks up.

                    ALBERTO
          What's the news, Wolf?

                    WOLF
          You tell me.

                    ALBERTO
          We're running a piece on Macy's.
          The protest is still on, right?

WOLF
You bet. What do you hear from
home?

ALBERTO
It's not good. There will likely be
a military coup any day, and I'm
afraid the socialist militias will
turn a civil war into a Revolution.

WOLF
You say that like it's a bad thing?

ALBERTO
You know as well as I do that a
revolution will pull in the
Stalinists.

WOLF
Yes. And the Nazis and Italians
will join the fight as well,
causing an international crisis.
And that, my friend, will force
people to take a stand. That will
lay the ground-work for a
successful Revolution.

ALBERTO
You have more faith in your country
than I do if you think the U.S.
will get involved. As long as it's
only Spanish boys who will die,
France and Britain will also keep
their distance. Neither a civil war
nor a revolution in Spain are
winnable. Why do you think I got

55

out? When Hitler and Mussolini join
the fight on the side of Franco...

MAX, the well-dressed editor in his late 30s, approaches
Alberto's desk.

> MAX
> Unless you join forces with the
> rest of the staff, Alberto, we're
> not getting this issue out. Wolf.

> WOLF
> Max.

> MAX
> We're going to run that piece you
> wrote on the Nazi Party recruiting
> in America.

> WOLF
> It's time we took the bastards on
> directly. In fact, that's exactly
> what we aim to do at Macy's.

> MAX
> It needs to remain peaceful, Wolf.
> Remember, this is about politics,
> not violence.

> WOLF
> Tell that to our comrades in
> Europe. This Hitler fellow will be
> responsible for the next Great War,
> and then plenty of people will
> learn the difference between
> violence and politics.

MAX

I despise the Nazis as much as you
do Wolf, but we need to be smart.
Violence now could ruin everything.

WOLF

Are you letting the staff off so
they can picket with us?

MAX

I've got a newspaper to get to
press. You know the way it works.

WOLF

Yeah. I know the way it works.

MAX

Jesus, Wolf. We've been over this.
It takes both guys in the trenches
and guys like us that put the guys
in the trenches.

WOLF

Actions speak louder than words.

An awkward silence.

MAX

Just don't get yourself arrested,
alright?

Max turns and goes back to his office.

ALBERTO

Maybe you shouldn't be so hard on
the old man. We're on the same
side, you know, and he's done a

hell of a lot for the Cause.

                    WOLF
I know. It's just his answer is
always politics. His unwillingness
to act sometimes really eats at me.

                    ALBERTO
You've heard the stories about Max
when he was younger, haven't you?
He was, no doubt, a man of action.
Speaking of action, you and Laura
seemed pretty friendly at the
meeting last night.

                    WOLF
Well you know as well as I do that
she's married.

                    ALBERTO
Well I think you need to get
yourself a girl, Wolf. This is
America after all.

EXT. MACY'S - DAY

Well-dressed immigrant workers picket. Signs read: "Long Live
the International Ladies Garment Workers Union", "Stop the
Nazis-Boycott Macy's" and "Macy's Buys German Products".
Police, some mounted, look disparagingly at the picketers.
LAURA, an attractive young woman, approaches.

                    WOLF
Laura! I'm glad you made it.

LAURA
I don't see you enough these days,
and I know this is important.

A red-faced GERMAN MAN runs out of the building screaming in
German. A POLICEMAN steps between the man and the picket
line. The mood is tense. The German man backs away.

LAURA (CONT'D)
The police will protect us, right?

WOLF
Police protect property.

A couple of well-dressed men jeer from across the street.

WELL-DRESSED MAN #1
Commies!

WELL-DRESSED MAN #2
Go back to Mother Russia!

LAURA
Maybe you should call off the
protest before something happens.

PICKETER
(at GERMAN MAN)
Squarehead!

POLICEMAN
(to PICKETER)
Shut your mouth, Beanie.

The German man smiles arrogantly at the picketer.

Nazi pig!

The German man lunges at the picketer. They fall exchanging
blows. Others rush in. Police wield batons. A MOUNTED
POLICEMAN cuts between Laura and Wolf. The horse's nostrils
flare. Laura stumbles backward into a different policeman.

POLICEMAN
Watch it, Lady!

WOLF
Leave her alone! She's not...
The policeman brandishes his baton at Wolf.

POLICEMAN
Step back, Mister!

Laura turns to run but slams into the side of the horse. The
mounted policeman raises his baton. Laura raises her arms as
the baton arcs down at her. At the last moment, Wolf throws
himself between the baton and Laura. Darkness.

INT. WOLF'S APARTMENT, BEDROOM - LATER

Wolf's eyes open slowly. His head is bandaged. He is in pain.
Stacks of books and socialist newspapers make the cramped
apartment appear smaller. Trotsky's picture hangs on the
wall. Laura enters. She places a hand on his forehead.

WOLF
What happened?

LAURA
You saved my life.

                    WOLF
          Was it bad?

                    LAURA
          It turned into a riot.

                    WOLF
          Is everyone okay?

                    LAURA
          Shhhh...You need to rest, Wolf.
Wolf reaches for Laura's hand.

                    WOLF
          They were there because of me.
Laura hesitates. Wolf squeezes her hand.

                    LAURA
          Eduardo and Ari were taken to the
          hospital. Ari is the worst off.
          They think he'll make it. Eli and
          Mikhail were arrested.

Wolf turns his face toward a black and white photograph of
two people standing in front of the Statue of Liberty.

                    WOLF
          This isn't the America my parents
          sacrificed so much to come to. I
          should've called the protest off.

                    LAURA
          You mustn't say that. You're always
          telling us we must act.

> WOLF

But look what happened.

> LAURA

Say not the struggle not availith,
Wolf. How many times have you told
us that? You have shown me more
than any other person I've met that
one man can make a difference. You,
Wolf, are the one who has shown us
what is possible.

> WOLF

I...

> LAURA

Shhh. Now you must rest. I insist.

INT. WOLF'S APARTMENT, LIVING ROOM - LATER

The radio is on. Laura is reading a newspaper. There is a
knock at the door. Laura opens the door revealing Max.

> MAX

How is he?

> LAURA

He's sleeping.

> MAX

Is it bad?

> LAURA

The doctor said he was lucky.

MAX

He's going to get killed one of
these days. He's not a soldier.

Max sits at the table and opens his briefcase.

MAX (CONT'D)

Did you hear about Spain?

LAURA

No. Is there news?

Max looks at his watch.

MAX

Turn up the radio. The newscast
should be coming on shortly.

Laura turns up the radio. There is a period Coca-Cola
commercial, and then it goes to the newscast.

BROADCASTER

This is Walter Winchell in New York
with a special news bulletin. We
are hearing reports that the
Spanish army seized control of key
government buildings throughout the
country in an apparent coup against
the socialist government. While
the army is reporting they have
been victorious in overthrowing the
democratically elected government,
it's clear they have not fully
silenced the opposition, even as
word of wholesale arrests and
rumors of summary executions
abound. Generalissimo Franco, who

appears to be leading the coup, has
declared victory, saying the people
of Spain would be better off under
his rule, a regime, he went on to
say, based on bayonets and blood
instead of hypocritical elections.

Wolf comes through the door from the bedroom.

LAURA
Wolf! You shouldn't be...

Wolf holds his hand up. He listens.

BROADCASTER
The Spanish anarchists, socialists
and communists are saying it will
be all out Civil War. Andre Nin, a
prominent member and founder of the
socialist political party known as
POUM has stated in a telegram to
the world press: "The Resistance in
the form of the militias will lead
the struggle to liberate Spain from
all Fascists in Europe." He
delivered an impassioned speech
over the radio urging all free
thinking peoples of Spain and the
world to unite in action and oppose
the coup. He ended his speech with
a call to arms: "Viva la Causa!" In
other news...

Laura turns the radio down.

WOLF
God damnit, that's it! I'm going.

LAURA
Going where?

WOLF
To Spain.

MAX
For Christ's sake, Wolf!

WOLF
I'm serious.
LAURA
But...
WOLF
Aren't you the one who just told me
I was right for acting?

LAURA
That was different, Wolf.

MAX
You've never been outside New York,
let alone fired a weapon.

WOLF
The same could have been said
about...

Wolf suddenly stumbles and catches himself on the arm of a
chair. Laura and Max both rush to his side.

MAX
You need to get back in bed.

Wolf looks at Max and then at Laura.

                    WOLF
            Maybe you're right.

Max walks Wolf back into the bedroom.

                    WOLF (O.S.) (CONT'D)
            I'm serious about Spain though...

                    MAX (O.S.)
            We'll talk about it later.

INT. WOLF'S APARTMENT - MORNING

Max is asleep on the couch. The first light of morning creeps
in. Max stirs. A stack of papers fall from his chest to the
floor, including a photograph with worn edges showing Max as
a young man screaming at a police officer over a barricade
with striking workers in the background. Wolf enters.

                    WOLF
            Did you sleep here?

                    MAX
            I guess I did.

Max sits up, straightening his clothes. He tucks the
photograph into his pocket before Wolf can see it.

                    MAX (CONT'D)
            How do you feel?

                    WOLF
            Like a stunned ox. I'll make coffee.

                    MAX
          You're certainly as stubborn as
          one. Sit. I'll make the coffee.

INT. WOLF'S APARTMENT - LATER

Wolf and Max sit at the table having coffee.

                    MAX
          So what happened out there
          yesterday? I thought you had
          everyone in line.

                    WOLF
          The police were looking for an
          excuse.

                    MAX
          The evening paper said Ari
          threatened Mr. Mueller.

                    WOLF
          Who... Oh. That's the Nazi's name.

                    MAX
          Did you see what happened?

                    WOLF
          Yeah. That Nazi bastard came
          running out of the building like a
          lunatic. If anyone threatened
          anyone, it was Mueller, not Ari. It
          doesn't surprise me the capitalist
          establishment papers didn't print
          it that way though.

                    MAX
          We can't afford this kind of press.
          Not now. Not when we are trying to
          unite the left and be taken
          seriously as a political force.

Wolf gets up and goes into the kitchen.

                    WOLF (O.S.)
          You know how I feel about joining
          forces with the communists, Max.

                    MAX
          Trotsky himself has called for the
          left to unite.

INT. WOLF'S APARTMENT, KITCHEN - CONTINUOUS

Wolf turns on the tap and rolls up his sleeves. He carefully
removes the bandage revealing a nasty gash on his forehead.

                    WOLF
          Are you forgetting the communist
          party threw us out on our asses
          over Trotsky?

Wolf cups his hands under the water and vigorously washes his
face. Turning the tap off, he grabs a towel.

INT. WOLF'S APARTMENT, LIVING ROOM - CONTINUOUS

Wolf dries his face and gingerly touches his wound.

                    WOLF
          I'm not getting why we'd join
          forces with those flunkies now.

Hummingbird Review

                         MAX
              It's already been decided, Wolf.

                        WOLF
              So now you just take orders?

                         MAX
              This goes to the top of the party,
              but I agree. It's never been more
              important for the left to project a
              unified front.

                        WOLF
              By playing at bourgeois politics?
              That won't help the worker enslaved
              by fascism or capitalism. Damn it,
              we are revolutionaries! If we are
              serious about opposing the fascist
              pricks, we must oppose them with
              guns not politics. Politics is no
              match for bayonets and blood.

                         MAX
              Damn it, Wolf. Sometimes you can be
              so fucking naive.

Max stands and collects his things.

                    MAX (CONT'D)
              I've got a deadline.

EXT. CENTRAL PARK - DAY
The sun is out. Couples walk hand-in-hand. Families picnic.
Laura and Wolf approach a pond where boys are sailing boats.

SUPER: Several weeks later.

                    LAURA
            What's eating you? You've barely
            said a thing all morning.

                    WOLF
            I got a letter this morning denying
            my request for a visa.

                    LAURA
            Good.

                    WOLF
            I'm going to find a way to get to
            Spain. I swear it. I can't stay
            here with these people who are
            oblivious to the fact Franco is
            massacring whole villages.

They approach an ice cream cart.

                    LAURA
            You know I believe in you, Wolf.
            You're the bravest, most honorable
            man I've ever met, and you've been
            such a leader for our group, but
            you're not a soldier.

                    WOLF
            Not yet.

                    LAURA
            You're incorrigible.

Wolf sees a group of people on the far side of the pond
gathered around two men in khaki uniforms with swastika
armbands handing out flyers. Wolf starts toward them.

LAURA (CONT'D)
Where are you going?

WOLF
Wait here.

Wolf walks toward the men. He sees a discarded flyer on the
ground and picks it up. Laura catches up. Wolf stares at the
image on the flyer: a uniformed man with a swastika armband
saluting George Washington in front of an American flag. It
reads: "PRO-AMERICAN RALLY. MASS DEMONSTRATION
FOR TRUE AMERICANISM AT MADISON SQUARE GARDEN".

LAURA
Is this for real?

WOLF
As real as it gets.

INT. THE MILITANT OFFICES - DAY

Wolf enters the office through a glass door where the words
THE MILITANT are being stripped from the glass. He has the
flyer in his hand. Alberto looks up.

ALBERTO
Wolf! It's good to see you.

WOLF
Where's Max?

ALBERTO
In his office, but...

Wolf storms across the room. He enters the office
without knocking.

INT. MAX'S OFFICE - CONTINUOUS

> **WOLF**
> So it's already happened?

> **MAX**
> I told you we were joining with the communist paper.

> **WOLF**
> So you're still playing politics?

> **MAX**
> I don't have the energy to fight with you right now, Wolf.

> **WOLF**
> Even with this?

Wolf slaps the flyer down on Max's desk.

> **MAX**
> Jesus.

> **WOLF**
> Hitler and Mussolini are backing Franco, and our Spanish comrades are being executed in the streets. And now the fucking Nazi party is recruiting in Central Park.

> **MAX**
> I know it's bad, Wolf, but what do you want me to do? Remain independent of the social-democrats

and the communists? Wage our own
revolution?

                    WOLF
You know as well as I do that
revolutions are the only way to
fundamentally change a society.

                    MAX
We've been at this a long time, and
what have we got to show for it?

Max stands and walks to the window.

                    MAX (CONT'D)
Maybe gradual democratic change can
achieve our ends in America.

Wolf is shaking, he's so angry.

                    WOLF
It's too damn easy for us to talk
politics. Don't you see that? You
must! What about where it matters?
What about our comrades in Spain?
They want what we do: freedom from
bourgeois oppression. Basic rights.
I can sure as hell tell you they'll
not achieve that through gradual
democratic change. They'll all be
dead unless someone acts!

                    MAX
                (exacerbated)
Then go to Spain, Wolf. Pick up a
gun and fight with the workers. Go.

Join the fighting in the streets.
Be part of the chaos and disorder.
You, the Jewish journalist from New
York who has never fired a gun,
will make a profound difference,
don't you think?

Wolf hesitates. He shakes his head, clearly disgusted.

                    WOLF
          What happened to you, Max?

                    MAX
          Come off it, Wolf.

                    WOLF
          Fuck you.

Wolf turns and exits the office.

INT. THE MILITANT OFFICES HALLWAY - CONTINUOUS

Wolf storms into the hallway. Alberto follows.

                    ALBERTO
          Wolf! Wolf! Wait a minute.

Wolf turns around. He is red in the face, angry as a hornet.
                    WOLF
          What?

                    ALBERTO
          I heard you and Max arguing.

                    WOLF
          Damn right!

ALBERTO
Let me buy you a coffee.

INT. COFFEE SHOP - LATER

Alberto and Wolf are seated at a table drinking coffee.

ALBERTO
What I'm saying is I left Spain
because I saw what was going on,
and I realized I could do much more
for the Cause by writing for Max
then taking potshots at fascists
from behind a barricade in a
Barcelona street.

WOLF
I understand what you're saying,
and I'd be lying if I said going to
Spain didn't scare me, but I could
have died a few weeks ago when a
policeman, someone who should be
protecting the people, clubbed me
like an animal. That changed
something in me, Alberto.

This is, I'm afraid, what the world
is coming to, and if nobody acts,
if nobody actually does something,
we'll all need to worry about more
than the fascists in Spain. Life is
uncertain. Given such uncertainty,
I don't have any choice.

ALBERTO
You're really serious, aren't you?

WOLF
Sure as Columbus discovered
America.

ALBERTO
You know Columbus didn't actually
discover America, right?

WOLF
I'm going to Spain.

Alberto looks at Wolf, as if he is studying him.

ALBERTO
I don't think you understand what
you'd be getting yourself into, but
I do admire your convictions.

Alberto pauses again. He is choosing his words carefully.

ALBERTO (CONT'D)
If you decide to go, if that's even
possible, I can help. The U.S. is
not issuing Spanish visas, and the
borders are closed under the
Neutrality Act, but I have friends
who can help you get to Barcelona
and connect with the POUM militia.

Wolf's face suddenly changes. He smiles broadly.

WOLF
I don't know what to say, Alberto.

Hummingbird Review

You're a good friend. So what do I
need to do?

Alberto leans in and starts talking in hushed tones.

                    WOLF (CONT'D)
EXT. ROOFTOP - NIGHT

Wolf and Laura exit a party in an apartment, making their way up
to the rooftop and a view of the city lights. It's hot. Laura has been
crying. Wolf tries to lighten the mood.

                    WOLF
              Thanks for organizing this send off
              for me, Laura.

                    LAURA
              I don't know what to do with you,
              Wolf. How can you be the most
              brave, beautiful, upstanding man on
              Earth and the most foolish,
              stubborn person at the same time?

                    WOLF
              You're the one that told me to act.

                    LAURA
              Yes! In a protest on the streets of
              New York. Not a trench in Spain!

                    WOLF
              Nothing will happen to me, Laura.

Laura stands up angrily and turns her back to Wolf.

                    LAURA
            Don't say that to me, Wolf
            Kupinsky. Don't lie to me.

                    WOLF
            I'll be careful. I promise.

Laura turns around. Her face is awash. She looks like she
might either hit him or hug him.

                    WOLF (CONT'D)
            Believe me, Laura, I'm scared.
            Honestly? I don't know if I can do
            this. I've never left New York,
            much the less touched a gun. This
            is the craziest thing I have ever
            considered doing. Maybe the
            stupidest. But I can't remain here
            and do nothing. I just can't. You
            understand that. I know you do.

She looks at him hard a moment and then hugs him.

                    LAURA
            You will make us proud, Wolf. I
            know that, but I'm scared for me. I
            know I might lose you. You need to
            know I believe in you. I always
            believe in you.

Wolf slowly return her embrace. The stars shine bright.

                    WOLF
            We should go back. People may talk.

> LAURA

Let them.

EXT. NEW YORK PIER - DAWN

The sun rises over the river. A hulking French freighter is moored at the pier. A bus stops. Dock workers, along with Wolf, disembark. Wolf carries a small bag. He hesitates for a moment, dwarfed by the immensity of the freighter's rusting prow. He compares the name on the bow with a sheet of paper from his pocket. He takes a deep breath and strides toward the gangplank. A taxi screeches to a stop. Max appears.

> MAX

Wolf! Wolf!

Wolf stops and turns around. Max jogs over to Wolf's side.

> MAX (CONT'D)

Sorry I missed your send-off.

> WOLF

I didn't expect you'd come.

> MAX

Listen, Wolf. We may have our differences, but I am your friend.

Max looks from Wolf's small bag up to the freighter's bow.

> MAX (CONT'D)

So this is it?

> WOLF

This is it.

                         MAX
                I wanted to say something.

Wolf looks anxiously at his watch.

                     MAX (CONT'D)
                I'll be quick. The thing is, Wolf,
                I look at people like you, and I
                see myself ten years ago. I admire
                your youth, your convictions. I
                admire them for a lot of reasons,
                but perhaps I admire them most
                because, in the darkest hours of
                the night as I lie awake, I fear,
                with the passing of my youth, has
                come the inevitable compromising of
                my convictions. And I hate that.

The freighter's horn sounds and dock workers start attending
to the lines. Wolf looks anxious.

                     MAX (CONT'D)
                I know you need to go, but I wanted
                you to hear that from me. I wanted
                you to hear that I admire you.

Max takes a large envelope from his coat pocket.

                     MAX (CONT'D)
                I have prepared these for you.

                         WOLF
                Pray tell?

                         MAX
                Your papers. Mr. Calverton has

approved your position as our chief
Spanish correspondent.

                    WOLF
          I'm going to fight, not write.

                    MAX
          Don't you think I know that? Give
          me a little credit. Getting into
          Spain won't be easy. Once you're
          there, staying out of trouble will
          be doubly hard. This letter
          authorizing you as our reporter may
          come in useful. And there's this.

Max takes another smaller envelope from his other pocket.
Wolf opens it. A small photograph of Trotsky playing with two
dogs falls out. Max picks it up and hands it to Wolf.

                 MAX (CONT'D)
          Everything you need to have the
          best chance of getting into Spain
          and meeting up with the socialist
          militia in Barcelona is in there.

Wolf is clearly moved.

                    WOLF
          I don't know what to say, Max.

                    MAX
          I do. I know you're going to Spain
          to fight, but this is going to be
          messy. Americans are going to have
          a hard time knowing the truth.

That's going to be your job, Wolf.
You are going to tell it like it
is, and we're going to publish it.

Max offers Wolf his hand. Wolf pulls Max close and hugs him.

                    MAX (CONT'D)
          Good luck, my friend, but even more
          important, viva la Causa, Comrade!

EXT. MARSEILLE, DOCK - NIGHT

Wolf steps off the gangplank of a rusting French freighter.
He carries a small bag. A ship's horn blows ominously as two
large rats scurry across the dock. It is raining lightly.

SUPER: Marseille, France. Several Weeks Later.

A flash of headlights from a nearby dark alley. Wolf
nervously approaches. The dock is poorly lit with an unsavory
air bordering on criminal. A dockworker in the shadows lights
a cigarette. Wolf startles. Quickening his pace, Wolf reaches
the driver's door of a WWI-era Mercedes flatbed truck.

                    BLACK DOG
          You're Alberto's friend?

                    WOLF
          Yes. I have papers...

Wolf fumbles to open his suitcase and take out the letter
given him by Max. He spills some of his clothes onto the damp
pavement in the process. BLACK DOG looks on impatiently.

                    BLACK DOG
          Just get in, for Christ's sake.

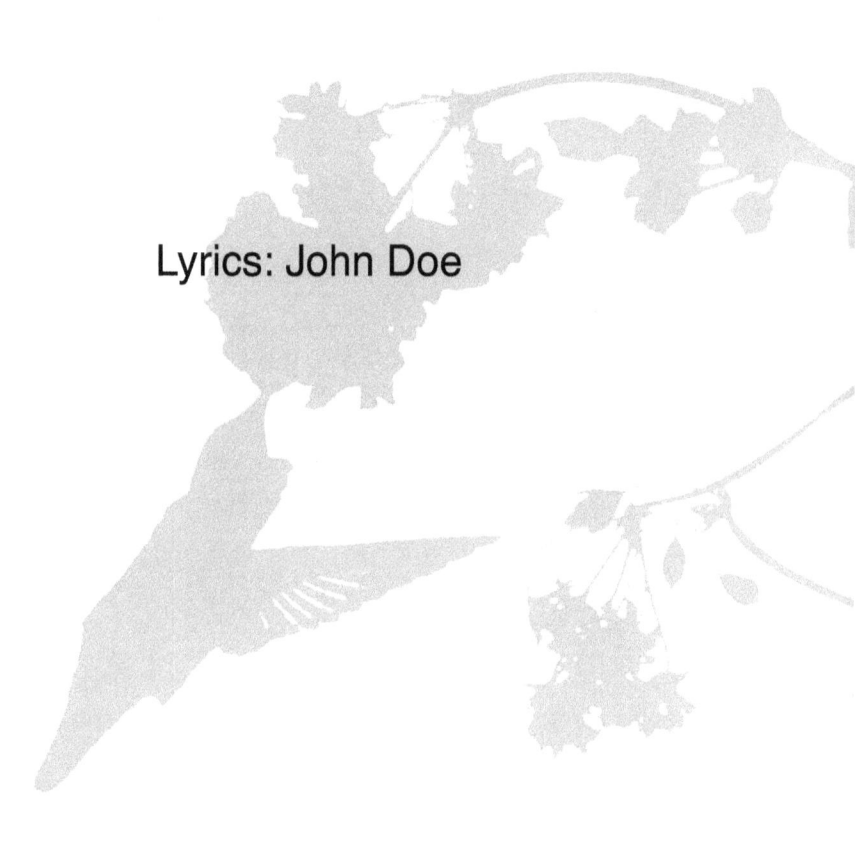

Lyrics: John Doe

Millions of punk and rock music fans know John Doe as the stylish, hard-driving singer/songwriter of the legendary L.A. punk/rockabilly group X. Doe and his cohort with X, Exene Cervenka, created a back-and-forth singing approach with their tough, hard-hitting lyrics that painted a picture of honest discontent while exposing the difficulties faced by, to use the title of one of X's greatest songs, "The Have-Nots." However, on X's *Live at the Whisky A Go Go* album, John hints at a deeper influence when he introduces he and Exene to the crowd as "Ma and Pa Kettle."

While X still tours, 35 years after its formation, John has branched out his talents, blending together an abiding love of the traditional west, its themes and stories, with singing, songwriting, acting and poetry writing. He has appeared in more than 30 motion pictures and 20 television series, including *Salvador* (1986), *Road House* (1988), *Great Balls of Fire!* (1989), *Wyatt Earp* (1994), *Boogie Nights* (1997), *Brokedown Palace* (1999) and *Wuthering Heights* (2003).

During the first *Hummingbird Review* launch reading in October 2010, we received a special surprise. John attended the event along with featured reader Michael Blake *(Dances with Wolves),* and we put him on the podium to read two of his original poems. Now, we present some of his finest lyrical work, just the way he likes it – raw and direct, letting the words tell the story. Three pieces are his own, while *Darling Underdog* and *The Have-Nots* are X songs, co-written by he and Exene.

JOHN DOE

A Little More Time

there was a time when the sunshine
played in your soft blonde hair
reflected in your golden eyes
you leaned back your head & you laughed
about tomorrow
and then it came, like a new day
the sun in the sky high beamed
water sparkled down the stream
we knew this would all go away
but not today
and when it did you were better
better than the day you were born
not quite so perfectly formed
the only wish I had that day
that it would stay
   just a little more time
   with you with me with you
down by the stream, in the mountains
I promised you faithfully
that I would never leave
if & when I went away, I'd still protect you
but now I'm gone & the loose ends
are stlngs hanging from my hands
tied to an empty land
stuck on a steering wheel in Nebraska
but I'm around so baby call me
just before you go to bed
before you lay down your head
or if you need an old fashioned cry, I'm the guy
   just a little more time
   with you with me with you
   just a little more time with you with me

Darling Underdog

green into blue
black into white
me into you
like ultra-violent light
feed me the songs
forgive me, I was wrong
darling underdog
disappearing in the fog
   traffic lights forever changing
   red to greenish-blue
   paper eyes
   your secret side
   underground w/ you
lunar disco ball
gospel delta light
down the lazy hall
kissing you goodnight
gone from lover's lane
to lovers' leap in pain
when I thought I could fly
you became the sky

Grain of Salt

that grain of salt
you talk about
gets bigger & bigger each day
it's making a pearl
inside my heart
w/ layers & layers of tears
I'd give you this pearl
to save our hearts
to keep them from bursting a vein
  my only hope
  is that someday soon
  you'll press your palm to my chest
  & the warmth of your hand
  will draw out the stone
  that wakes me every night
I give you this pearl
to show my love
I've grown it for over a year
& if I'm true then maybe you
will take me along with the jewel

The Golden State

you are the hole in my head
I am the pain in your neck
you are the lump in my throat
I am the aching in your heart
we are tangled
we are stolen
we are living
where things are hidden
you are something in my eye
I am the shiver down your spine
you are the lick of my lips
I am on the tip of your tongue
we are tangled
we are stolen
we are buried up to our necks in sand
  we are luck
  we are fate
  we the feeling you get in the golden state
  we are love
  we are hate
  we are the feeling I get when you walk away
you are the dream in my nightmare
I am that falling sensation
you are my needles & pins
I am your hangover morning

The Have Nots

have a drink at the Bar Nothing,
bar anything
but the bottom step of the ladder
It keeps getting higher & higher

dawn comes soon enough
for the working class
it keeps getting
sooner or later
This is the game
that moves as you play

How does it feel
to have your own bottle of booze
behind the bar, how does it feel?
to play cards w/ the barmaids while they work

at Jocko's Rocketship and
the One Eyed Jacks
My Sin & the Lucky Star
a steady place to study & drink

dawn comes soon enough
for the working class
it keeps getting
sooner or later
This is the game
that moves as you play

Day old days
   ancient
bloody mary bastards
in a hardcore blue collar bar
here we sit, a shot & a beer
after another hard earned day

dawn comes soon enough
for the working class
it keeps getting
sooner or later
This is the game
that moves as you play

at the Hi-Di-Hi & the Hula Gal, the Beehive Bar and the Zircon Lounge,
G.G.'s Cozy Corner, the Gift of Love, Stop'N'Drink, Sit'N'Sip,
Rest'N'Pieces
Dexter's New Approach and the Get Down Lounge,
The Aorta Bar, *Detroit's main vein*
Art's Magic Moment, Hee Haw Bar, Charlie's Angels Lounge
El Inferno, Baby Doll's Polka-dot Bar,
Don't Ask, Club Super Fly, Fun Box,
Lucy's Wisconsin Rendezvous, Who Cares, Midget's Nite Life
The Salvage Yard, Slammer Inn & the Swamp

Dawn comes soon enough for the working class
it keeps getting sooner or later
This is the game that moves as you play

Remembering Bill Studebaker

ROBERT YEHLING

Salute to Bill Studebaker

The first time I met Bill Studebaker, he engaged in an Amazon blow dart fight at midnight, played Gene Autry records circa 1930, and showed photos of he and his son kayaking in a Greenland fjord, as well as plunging down a waterfall – and making it. Not exactly what you'd expect at a Twin Falls, Idaho party on New Year's Eve. His lovely wife, Judy, smiled and shook her head. Boys will be boys. Bill also tried to talk me into kayaking down the nearby Snake River the next morning – in 5-degree weather. "Good way to start the New Year," he said.

I shivered at the thought. "Uhhhh … No thank you."

What a first impression. I attended the party to ring in 2002 and meet one of my favorite poets, only to run into his other persona – a crazy adventure seeker. Yet, what will last forever is the voice of Idaho's Poet Laureate Emeritus, a master of lyric verse whose dozen collections weave together love, place, water, nature, change, western lore, hardy small towns, and eclectic individuals. Fittingly, his last work was *About a Place Called Home*. He served terms on the Idaho Writers' Connection, the Idaho Commission on the Arts, and the Idaho Humanities Council. In 2005, he received the state's Outstanding Achievement in the Humanities Award. He also edited *Idaho's Poetry: A Centennial Anthology*. In my eyes, he belongs in an elite group of western poets alongside Gary Snyder, Robinson Jeffers, Robert Duncan, Michael McClure, Joy Harjo, N. Scott Momaday, Kenneth Rexroth, and Jimmy Santiago Baca.

Bill and I stayed in touch, comparing new poems or discussing workshops we taught. I asked for a tip or two from the College of Southern Idaho professor. Always, I would also ask, "Where did you go on your latest kayaking adventure?" I knew that question would draw an impassioned, effusive answer – every time.

We last touched base in 2007. A year later, on July 4, 2008, he died at age 61 in a kayaking accident on the East Fork of the

South Fork of the Salmon River, near Yellow Pine. He died on 5+ rapids (the highest difficulty) – his favorite kind of ride.

Bill loved the magic, discovery and innocence of true adventure. Fittingly, a magical event took place after his passing. "Divers looked for him for ten days but couldn't find him," Judy Studebaker recalls. "My daughter and son-in-law kept looking; my daughter wouldn't stop until she found him.

"Then a hummingbird flew in front of her face. She told me, 'It felt like he was staring me down.' She felt guided to go downriver. She, my son-in-law and Shane Harper, a kayaking buddy who'd flown in from Alaska after we'd texted him that Bill had drowned, headed a couple miles downriver. They looked out and saw something glinting in the river – Bill's knife. It was attached to his vest … which he was still wearing."

This story deepens. Bill and one of his best friends, archaeologist Jim Woods, studied the mythologies of indigenous peoples in North and South America. Studebaker gravitated to a specific belief of Central American tribes. "They believed hummingbirds took great warriors to the next world," Judy says. "Bill was a warrior in everything he did – kayaking, his poetry, the example he set. How wonderful was it that a hummingbird came and guided my daughter to find him? It was like he came and said, 'Everything's OK, let's own this.'"

When we contacted Judy through College of Southern Idaho professor Whitney Smith, and told her we wanted to salute Bill in *The Hummingbird Review,* she choked up. "I was so happy when I heard about this," she says. "Of all literary journals! You know, I'm surrounded by pictures of hummingbirds in my house, hummingbirds outside … the only thing I've lost is his physical presence."

Now, in the next six poems, in his own words, Idaho's greatest poet flies again.

BILL STUDEBAKER

About a Place Called Home

This is where the Gods
practice simple things
like up and down and forever.
The whole desert slopes casually
until it is far away, and the eye
sees every direction the same.
Name this place Anywhere,
and you are halfway there
when your head blows out
and you stop for water
in the middle of a dry lake
not knowing which shore
is the beginning
or which will be the end.
If you wait too long,
you will die of thirst,
and you can kiss the wind goodbye.
Keep going, and there you will be,
hanging to a clump of what's left,
a good dream
everyone else has given up on.

Signals

A second without pain
is eternity,
and so is the kiss
between lips of an open wound,
and when you discover
there is no forward
and when the engines
of silence sit idle,
pain will not be deaf,
but speaks the language of the deaf –
its hands screaming
words for wounds:
hatred, bullets, indifference, gas.
There will be one
monoxide moment
when you can
almost read the dark
smoke of poetry
gathering the tribes.

Blue Sky

Fairfield is the size of a matchbox,
laid out so unimaginatively
Main Street runs
perpendicular to traffic.
Every viable business
has turned its back on the town,
and the promise of subdivisions
has begun to collapse
where houses and homes might have been.
This is small-town everywhere
in the West. The postman
delivers less mail, the preacher
gives fewer sermons, the mortician
carries the dead to their graves
in a good used pickup.
Yet no one forgets that above them
is the blue sky they're all vested in.
Conversations are spoken with the eyes,
and follow you everywhere.
Every particle of posture is a point of gossip.
All news is old news
in a dialect encrypted with caution.
The town crier is an old dog—
black and white and wise about cows.
Her bark ignites the town pack
to a frenzy of yips and yowls.
Go around this town, and you're out of it.
Go out the backdoor, and you're in the country.

Stop, and silence is so profound
you'll forget why you thought of it.
Walk, and you'll feel a light weight
like a clear bubble about you.
That's when you'll understand
why you've come to invest in blue sky.

Sandpoint

Old Lady Weil
came here rough as an Iowa cob,
but the years pushed against her like waves,
wearing her skin smooth as the beach
she hobbles down to town.
And old man Deshon
sits in his '64 Ford
counting his four missing fingers,
remembering when he
set chokers with one hand.
So many dreams have drowned
in this lake. ...
The fish get bigger each year.
And tonight, a young logger
takes Old Lady Weil's granddaughter
out on the point,
holds her, raising his arm
with four good fingers
toward a fish rising
to swallow the white lure of the moon,
knotted to a string
buoyed to the rest of their lives.

Waiting Tables in Pomeroy

This town has fallen on such hard times
you have to pay to die. And if
you want to keep your mind,
they double the rent. Your grandmother,
the first town idiot, a woman
no one paid much mind, sang
a rosary of lost relatives.
(What do you care?
You were adopted anyway.)
Your job, waiting the last table
still open, has advantages.
You can give your customers tips,
steer them away from settling here.
As it is, there aren't enough men
nor women. Everyone seems to be
missing somebody. The locals' pockets
are full of counterfeit possibilities,
families forged when dreams were tender.
You've sold so much coffee for a yarn
you're loaded with muscles
from lifting skeletons and ghosts.
Like the ones about you:
you're your mother's youngest sister.
You're what's left of an idiot's menopause.
You're what's left after the rent
was doubled.
But there is ... just enough money
for one person to die at a time.

Ars Poetica

Every year they return.
They have no map
almost no brain.
They come anyway:

stealhead, chinook salmon
traveling in silence
toward spawning beds
up the clear stream
of death.

I have sat these years
rocking my soul
while the river tunes rocks
and the green voice
of the ocean plays back
a euphonious eulogy
to the waters of the world.

Everything goes without saying.
Like my fish
these lines will turn belly-up
in the headwaters
at the glacier's foot.

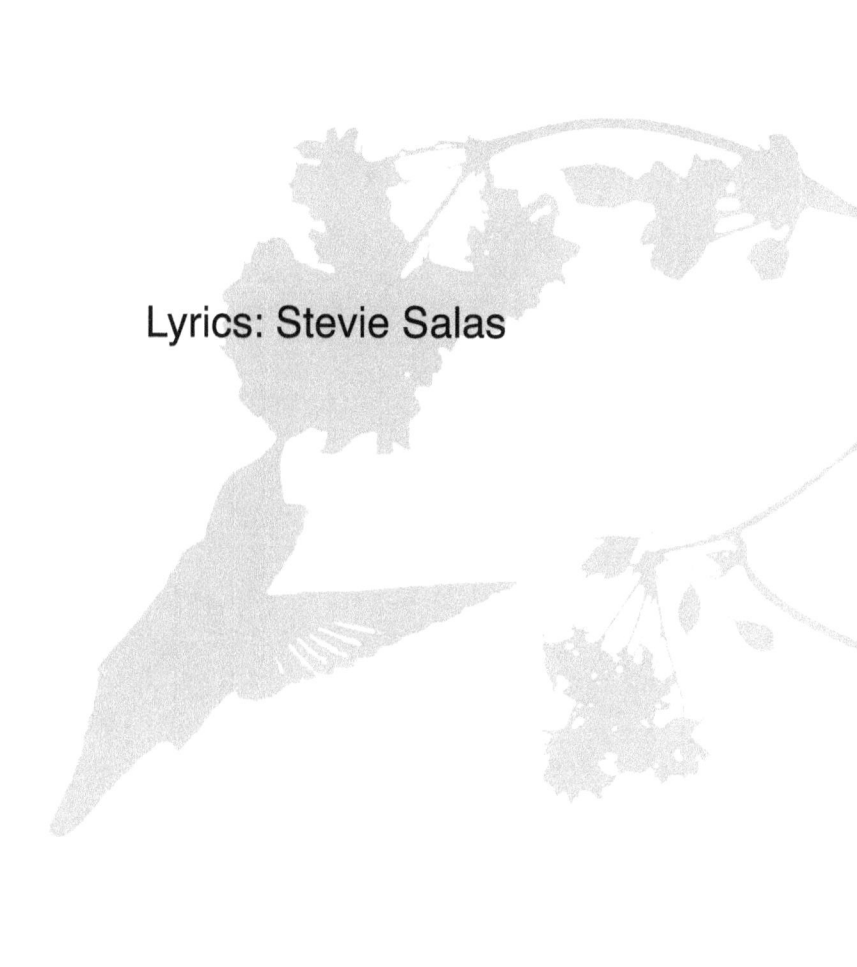

Lyrics: Stevie Salas

S tevie Salas' distinguished music career began with quite a leap. Within three years, he rocketed from playing small gigs and backyard parties in San Diego County to becoming Rod Stewart's "boy wonder" lead guitarist on the 1988 Out of Order world tour. He also scored the music for *Bill & Ted's Excellent Adventure*. Since then, he has appeared on or produced nearly 100 albums, toured with Mick Jagger and Terence Trent D'Arby on their solo excursions, headlined sellout tours of his own, and recorded ten albums with several million total sales. In 1990, *Guitar World* magazine named him the No. 3 new guitarist; *Guitar World* in Japan ranked him No. 1.

Today, Stevie is the Contemporary Music Advisor to the Smithsonian Institution. He and actor Adam Beach (*Law & Order: SVU, Flags of Our Fathers, Walker Texas Ranger*) are executive producers of *Arbor Live,* a music variety show and one of the top TV shows in Canada. Stevie is also producing a documentary on North American Indians in pop music, as well as working on his next album. Along with *The Hummingbird Review* editor Robert Yehling, Stevie is working on his memoir, When We Were The Boys, a coming-of-age story set against Rod Stewart's Out of Order Tour.

We asked Stevie to pull five songs from his wide body of music. He furnished the extra favor of writing out the backstories to each song.

STEVIE SALAS

Indian Chief
(From *Stevie Salas Colorcode*, 1990)
I always noticed that when people died, a song would come out, say-
ing how important they were and how much they were loved (I wish
I would have told you...did you know you were my hero, etc., etc.).
I always thought that was crazy, since the person was dead and not
around to hear it, so I wrote this song to my Father – who is still
very much alive.

He always was a hard working man,
working all his life for the things I had
He never asked me for nothing except to be a man
and that's what I tried to do
He always listened to the words I said and if
he didn't at least he'd pretend
I realize now what I didn't then he really is my best friend

Oh you are an Indian Chief to me
Yeah you are my Indian Chief
And I thank you

The Lord only knows just where I'd be probably
in jail or in the streets
But he turned me around with words I belleved
I owe so much to you
If I could I'd give you back your years and send
you to the country with all your friends
I'd bring all the living and bring back the dead
so you could have yourself a good time

Oh you are an Indian Chief to me
Yeah you are my Indian Chief
And I thank you

Like that river water running deep so runs my love for you
Like a desert rainstorm cools the heat I thank
the Lord for giving me to you

I'm not gonna wait until the day you die to say
these words that are on my mind
I figured you could dig it while you were still alive
and you'll know this was all for you

Oh you are an Indian Chief to me
Yeah you are my Indian Chief
And I thank you

The Lying Truth

(From *Back From The Living*, 1994)

I was really on a roll while making this record, but like most artists, I think I always had the feeling it was all for nothing...To be young and confident on the outside, while the constant fear of failure walks you down from within...

Drifting I'm falling I'm drowning so slowly
I'm failing with me Failing with you
Trying not doing I'm crawling not moving
I'm failing with me Failing with you

Breathing in water way over my head
Body's alive but emotions are dead
There's nowhere to go but there's places to hide
I promise to try but you know how I lie

Touching not feeling Not living just breathing
I'm failing with me Failing with you
Taking receiving Collapsing completely
I'm failing with me Failing with you

Walking a straight line that curves with no end
Five steps behind me then four steps ahead
Moving so slow that I'm going nowhere
My brain is well fried but my heart is still rare

I'm the living proof I'm the lying truth
I'm the lying truth

Alter Native

(From *Alter Native*, 1996)

I had been spending more and more time in Indian Country, trying to find a balance between my sex, drugs and rock 'n roll life and my search for my spiritual Native American self. I was also laughing a lot at the music business, because rock music went alternative. Overnight, I watched people change their images, cut off their hair and pretend they were punks. A lot of people switched from party-all-night lyrics to painful, dark and druggy lyrics. The insincerity was beyond belief. I was never in either group, but could roll with both, so I didn't run into this problem. For this song, I took the word 'alternative' and made a play with Alter Native, and talked about a mass exodus from rock by using stereotype words you might hear in an old western. It was a bit of fun!

True myths and a master plan help push the
bandwagon across the land
Burn my soul on sacred ground then burn me out
with the same old sound
Soaring high on borrowed wings and sinking
deep in the shallow steam
Alter Native

Wild mustangs on open plains, wild horse in your veins
Search the deep water for new ideas but to catch the big one
you got to fish the mainstream
God save the Alter Native

Sacred hair and ego to fill the sky now the hair is gone but oh my my
Similar thoughts in a changing time Greener thoughts of an earlier
time…when I could breath
Bye bye Alter Native

A Lullaby Of Wishes
(From *Shapeshifter*, 2001)

*In the spring of 2000, the love of my life died. She was with me on
and off since my first tour with Rod Stewart; I wrote many songs
about us. When I started the* Shapeshifter *record, so much pain and
anger came out. I don't listen to this record, because it was the worst
time in my life. Many years later, I was in Europe, and a French
woman asked me about 'A Lullaby of Wishes'. I hadn't really listened to it since it came out, and I had never played it live. She said
it always made her cry. She didn't know what I wrote it about, but it
affected her deeply. In 2012, I listened to this album with open ears
and this song did stand out. It's about my girl going to heaven and
the loneliness waiting for me.*

The sand across my heart's path blows with no
meaning no future no past
The lonesome wind can't bring back to life my once upon a time
In every ocean in every dream in every forest in every tree
On every mountain where sunlight explodes she's there I know

A lullaby of wishes when you fly to the Angels who set you free
A lullaby of wishes when you cry for the devil who cries for me

She paints the sky in soft pastels gone
are the clouds where her darkness dwelled :
Free at last the smallest brave has found her way
A lullaby for my Cherokee with heavy heart she had to leave
Light green eyes and deep blue grass she's home at last

A lullaby of wishes when you fly with the Angels who set you free
A lullaby of wishes when you cry for the devil who cries for me

What It Was To Be What It Is
(From *Be What It Is*, 2007)

After seven years of running from myself, I finally came back. I don't remember a lot about those seven years ... it's really strange. I did know that I was now was an old man in rock 'n roll years, but I still wanted to push the envelope and not live in my past. The music business was now overrun with people who couldn't play music. I wrote this song about learning to accept where I was, and who I am.

Everybody's rockin but don't know how a lot of
talk talk talk talking like they've been around
I gotta put it on blast when ever I don't believe
you know what I want yeah
you know what I bleed
Another bad mother *vato* trying to steal my sound
trying to be a wolf but chasing bitches like a hound
But sooner or later they all get found believe me
I know a thing about it

I said Hey
What it was to be what it is
You should have known me now instead of then
What it was to be what it is
Just be what it is

So what am I what am I what am I supposed to do
I used to be hot hot hot but now I'm cool with myself that is
And I don't think I'm lying but that don't mean
I'm ready for dying

I said Hey
What it was to be what it is
You should have known me now instead of then
What it was to be what it is
Just be what it is

Remind me to remember what I can't forget
that my money and my mind are already spent
But I'll keep on rockin', doin' what I please,
you know what I want yeah you
know how I bleed
So all you talk in suckers better check your mind
'Cuz you ain't got no choice this jam is amplified

I said Hey
What it was to be what it is
You should have known me now instead of then
What it was to be what it is
Just be what it is

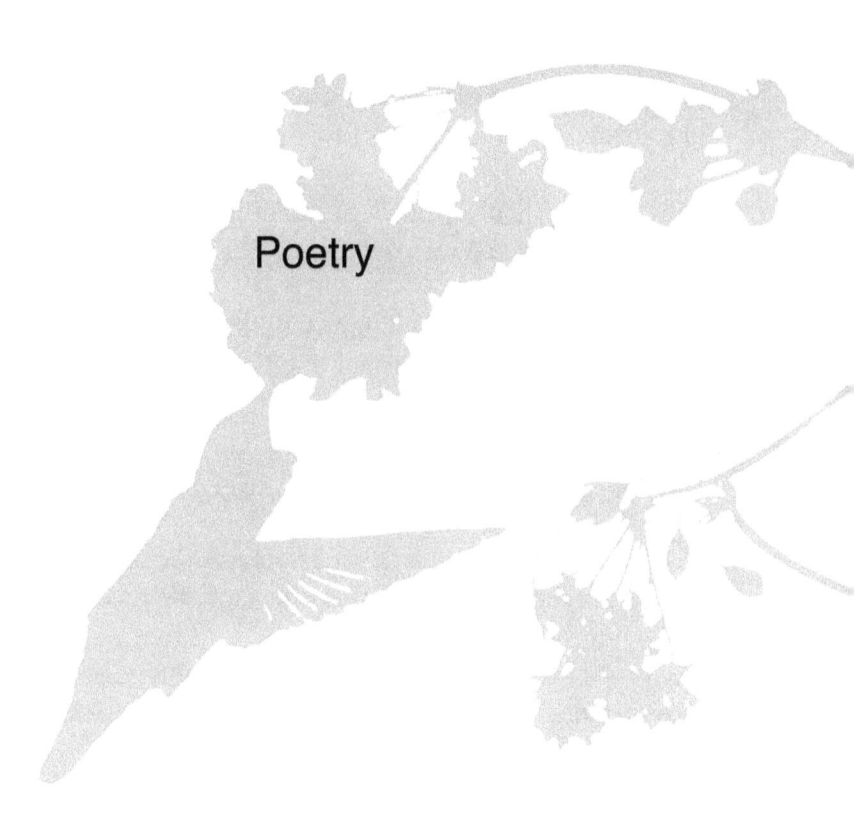

Poetry

RICKI MANDEVILLE

Soon, My Love

March

At the kitchen table, she sits and watches wind tie fluorescent
clouds around the moon, her breath against the cold window

shrouding the apple trees in false fog as they stand in her yard
like shadows of old men. A few persistent drifts of snow

hug the fence, a clear blade of moonlight slicing down,
honing itself on the refrozen crust. Her fingertips ache

with the stored cold of winter as, on the pane, she writes
Soon, my love, then wraps her hands around the steaming mug.

August

In the oven of August, sidewalks bake at the edge of her lawn;
a clear curtain of heat shimmers through the raised window.

She props both elbows on the table, thoughts scattering
like seed pearls: Yards of yellowed lace boxed in the stifling attic.

Her married daughter in Kentucky. Two grandsons.
Her Henry peaceful in the earth, holding her place the same way

he used to warm their bed, lying a while on her side,
sliding across when she slipped in. Soon, my love.

She pushes her chair back from the table, dissolves her loneliness
in lukewarm tap water, feeds it to the ivy, the browning fern,

RICKI MANDEVILLE

the drooping geranium on the window ledge where the calico
grooms its raised hind leg. Stiff fingers loosened by the heat,

she shines philodendron leaves with a soft cloth. Tends them
lovingly, as though they were family.

After Image
(after a photograph by Billie Bish Fargo)

Even when the window finally darkened,
even when the sky sank dregs
of twilight into silhouettes of pines

even when the last bird hushed its call
and stars hung frozen in sparse scatters
like yellow crumbs flung onto a black cloth

waiting for the earth to whisk them west
and I couldn't, in the blackness past the glass, see
treetops swaying (though I knew there was wind)

even when I pulled the covers smooth
and slipped myself between them, stalk of silk
in my white nightgown, I couldn't sleep,

the blaze of sunset still too vivid in my mind,
a holy fire that, while I watched, touched flame
to mountains, burned the clouds to ash.

ELLEN BEALS

Opossum

I vow to change,
start with the first bad habit,
and the opossum moves back into my yard.

This time it's for real, no giving in,
and that opossum makes a nest under my deck.

I've lived in my head way too long
and the opossum sets up house.

The dog is nuts for it,
chewing the wood to get at it,
venturing as far under as she can go.

She whines and whines at the opossum
and I can see its pale fur move between the slats.

Each spring I try to be better
and that opossum always comes back.

JOHN GARDINER

From Whence We Come

And in the end, the love we take is equal to the love we make.
–The Beatles

The turbulent blood we carry
in wild rivers of flesh and bone
was born in ponds of algae and mud.
Ireland and England circulate me,
a shamrock floating on the Thames.

When casting a stone into roiling water
to seek a lover from a billion souls,
the ripples going out are requests,
those coming in are replies.

All of us are mixed in the same broth,
and the marrow in our bones
from the great house of genes
is geared to find the love we need.

When we're not making love,
the ripples disappear

as does the river,
as does the pond.

In Patagonia

The old man selling canoes made of sea lion skin
is a pure-blooded Kawesquar.
His clothes are made of seal hide
and more than half his life has been spent

JOHN GARDINER

in one of these canoes, sleeping and cooking,
diving for mussels in the frozen fjords
of southern Chile, shadowed by the Andes
at the bottom of the world.

The old man knows his tribe is disappearing,
and the strange looks he gets from tourists
are nothing compared to the strange wonders
he has seen. When asked about the future,
he says: In our concept, the future doesn't exist.

Solace

Loathing most things human and dark with rage
after reading about fishermen
who lure and then slaughter thousands of dolphins
because they survive on fish the fishermen sell,
I stumbled outside at midnight
with a water pail
and stared at my garden
as if I were Willy Loman
ready to plant his doldrums
under a gloomy moon.

I took solace in my dogs,
and they kissed the black clouds away
with tongues of understanding,
eyes of diamond compassion;
one of them placed his cold nose in my ear
to calm the shrieking sounds of death
I couldn't stop imagining.

JOHN GARDINER

My dogs hark the arrival of south swells,
spell-bound, staring out to sea,
sensing perhaps the movements of other beings
and possessing no instinct
to add bloody histories of their own.

JENNIFER HILLMAN

Lover of Words

I am lover of words... I am wickedly drunk with the magic of words... the poetic nature whispers through and to my very heart and soul. As I dance with an intoxicating fever I can't deny, they move me like music of the stars, shining in the night skies.

Seduce me not with false promises and leading questions that twist words. Linger with me as the taste of sweet wine tingles on our tongues, dancing the essences of the charm of this moment's breath.

Capture me with tender words like the sweeping motion of the ocean, the breeze whipping me to frenzy. Quench my thirst with the subtleties of reason and passions divine.

Touch me tenderly, lingering in the quality of the statements. I dive in with light stepping elegance... devoid of expectation, yet my inquisitive mind bright for the moment.

Taste the motion of the waves of sensuality broken down with syllables and rhythms, pulling into the current and washing me with the stringing truth of the rawness of my soul.

That unnerving raw powerful expression... cutting through layers and levels of illusions and delusions of the mind, bringing to the surface nuances of intentions... devotion realized. The heart pounds with the releasing energies of doubtful uncertainties into the trust and truth revealed, open and raw, ripping off the mask with that passionate exchange of emotions and song.

This dance of words continues on...

CHARLES REDNER

From far Montana's cañons,
Lands of the wild ravine, the dusky Sioux, the lone-
some stretch, the silence,
Haply, to-day, a mournful wail—haply, a trumpet
note for heroes.
— Walt Whitman

When a Mighty Pen
Crossed a Bold Saber

Reading Walt Whitman describe
then trumpet the Battle
of the Little Big Horn—
I wonder if he felt
empathy for the dead Indians
or just for the dead cavalry.

Within days of the encounter,
the poet pens, "A Death-Sonnet For Custer."(1)
Here he extols the brave *Americans*,
refers to the Native Americans
as dark and shady, hiding in ambush,
prepared for a slaughter.
Did Whitman know it was Custer
who pursued the Indians?

Shakespeare would have lauded
Whitman's heroic description:
"… desperate and glorious—aye,
in defeat, most desperate, most glorious."
"… leaving behind thee a memory sweet
to soldiers. Thou yieldest up thyself."

CHARLES REDNER

Two years after the battle
the tableau spread before Whitman's eyes—
gifted by way of John Mulvany's
life-sized painting titled,
"Custer's Last Rally."(2)
The poet wrote again.

He describes: "swarms upon swarms
of savage Sioux ... like a hurricane of demons."
It was Kill Eagle, a Blackfoot Sioux chief
who first observed that the Indians
went at Custer's column, "like a hurricane
... like bees swarming out of a hive."
Once again, I ponder how Whitman
might have felt. Had new understanding
altered his sentiments?

Then a hint from Whitman's essay,
"... nothing in Homer, nothing in Shakspere [sic];
more grim and sublime than either,
all native, all our own ..."

Whitman witnessed war's scars up close at field hospitals
during the War Between the States—
did this painting ignite tortured memories?
Did he grieve only for the North's wounded and dead?

Whitman stroked his lengthy whiteness,
furrowed his brow and sat in silence
for over an hour staring at the painting.
How did he feel recalling all the young lives
of opposing sides, cut so short
at Manassas, Gettysburg, Antietam,
and now, The Little Big Horn?

CHARLES REDNER

A 1970s book by Dee Brown, (a title borrowed from Stephen Vincent Benet) *Bury My Heart At Wounded Knee*, describes the famous battle from the victor's vantage point. Brown was candid about his intention to present the history of the settlement of the West from the point of view of the Indians, "its victims," as he wrote. He noted, "Americans who have always looked westward when reading about this period should read this book facing eastward." Inspired by Brown, Michael Blake penned *Dances with Wolves*, a most sympathetic view of the plight familiar to all Native Americans since the first Europeans landed in "India." In 2007, *Dances with Wolves* was selected for preservation in the United States *National Film Registry* by the Library of Congress as being "culturally, historically, or aesthetically significant."

1. "A Death Sonnet for Custer," New York Daily Tribune, 10 July 1876, reprinted as "From Far Dakota Grass" (1881-82).
2. "Custer's Last Rally," Whitman's essay on painting of same name by John Mulvany.

ERICA GOSS

Salt to Salt

1.

At the lip of the Pacific
a shoe fills with sand.
It's a huge shoe, a man's shoe,
the size my father used to wear,

mass-produced in a country where
the people have small hands and feet.
Now it rocks in front of me
dilapidated, saturated

as the sea pulls boots of silt
up past my ankle bones. Maybe
I should let the beach absorb me

wait until the sand closes
over my head
while a sea lion regards me
with one innocent, chocolate eye.

2.

We dwell inside each other, salt to salt
yet the sea and I are strangers, opaque
as parents to their children.

Dead below the knees
my father watched continents drift
in and out of view
those big feet in lopsided running shoes.

In the end he forgot everything

ERICA GOSS

lost in that seductive vista:
islands, hazy peaks,
the water's sliding surfaces.

     3.
We are not finished –

a lone shoe
is the punch line to
some impenetrable joke

and me at the water's edge
ready for more uncanny gifts

while the sea
wearing an old coat
waits for its children
to come home.

ERICA GOSS

Boden

I know it's hard to love me;

crushed under cities
scraped from your shoes.

I want attention. I want
to live under fingernails
find my way into your mouth.

I give you monkey-flower, nettles,
the bay tree's rising scent.
I understand sacrament.

Spread a blanket over me.
I banish isolation.
Take your lover right here.

Lie down and listen:
the dead clot within me.
I could rouse them, but I won't.

I lift mountains over bones.
In the green grass of the field
take your rest in me.

CLAUDETTE MARCO

Beyond The Universe

Senses gone elsewhere
love and hope long disappeared
towards realm of space.

Shades of blue energy
pulsate from hull, planet, star;
exhilaration.

Senses perceive form
refreshing mind, doldrums, life;
deserves to be watched.

Watcher is taken
by story springing water,
awakening senses.

In a moment calm
hollow life changes wholly
towards a new journey.

Watcher sees hero,
water moves, quenching dry lake:
Unbelievable.

Where no heart remained
watcher hears a faint beating –
perspective transforms.

Could one really see
love, hope, and turn to blue
like the energy?

CLAUDETTE MARCO

Hero speaks of tales
and battles he won and lost,
yet no one listens.

Was it the villain
who persuaded all others?
Watcher does not care.

Hero steps aside
in a spaceship large and wide
Watcher hunts madly.

Story shades hero.
Comfort fills watcher's lake bed
to the height of stream.
Story shows people
all together, yet alone.
Watcher sees mirror.

People find courage –
when the ship is fixed but broken,
hope oozes and spurts.

"Find me the hero!"
declares the watcher in vain.
Life now has meaning.

Realization:
watcher perceives their story
through a detached screen

The Hero comes and goes
past indifference, sees flight,
heart and faith find growth.

CLAUDETTE MARCO

An hour is too short
Time strikes the watcher's grown heart
Two years is too short.

Watcher encounters
unfriendly, cold TV screen.
Eyes see beyond it.

All on the spaceship
live beyond the universe
in the Watcher's heart.

JOHN ROULEAU

Remind Me

Dear sister
in your alcoholic stupor
you drift into the fetid past
we shared as children

when i call
please
don't bring me back

there

remind me of the river
the change of seasons
the great migrations above us
we watched when so small
and innocent
and pure

remind me of crabapple trees
and plum
running from yard-to-yard
from dawn till dusk
with the neighbor kids

a long string of family dogs
and again

the river.

JOHN ROULEAU

At the Chinese Cemetery

At the Chinese cemetery
we visit Ming Ming's grandfather
during the season for remembering,
the smell of incense. Several generations
leave flowers and dumplings on headstones
and burn spirit money to send it on
to ancestors. In the columns of smoke,
like ashes, roiling
flecks of black and white –
seagulls and crows float
like ghostly shadows.

Keys Haiku

She knows I'm leaving
by the jangling of my keys.
"Bye daddy! Love you!"

two young soldiers
sit behind me
on the aircraft
like kids their arms
entwined
speaking

in whispers
as though muttering
prayers

NEFRETETE RASHEED

On the Last Day of the World

(Response to C. Eady)

On the last day of the world
I will be shaking my you know what
on somebody's dance floor

I will be wound up in
a sarong of music
I will be a drumbeat

A thud. a period
caught mid-sentence
On the last day

I will be belting it out in a tight
crowded room. I will be the *ooh baby ooh*
in that slow jam

I will be a reckless word
jumping off the page
A not so quiet storm

A star trek
traveling miles
in the last moment

To free every memory
caught in a photograph
every shadow subjugated by brightness

NEFRETETE RASHEED

And I will dance to the table
for the last supper
my initiation completed

My lessons learned:
I will dance on the table
At the last supper

On the last day of the world.

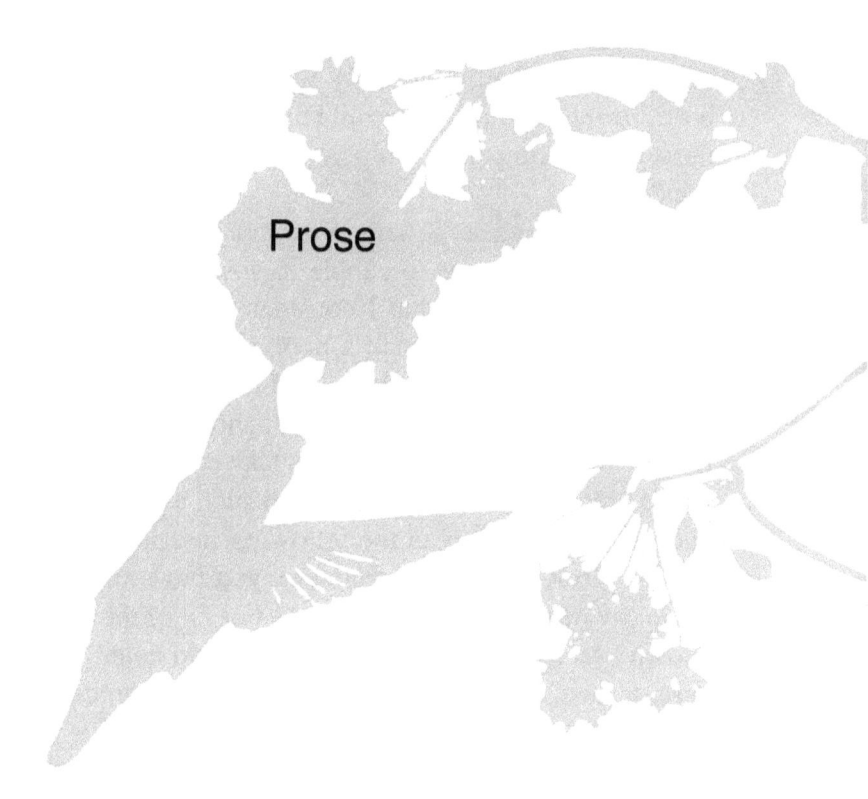

Prose

KATHRYN A. KOPPLE

My Beautiful Countess

Most honorable cousin,

No doubt, you will consider me a nuisance, writing to you after my first letter was returned unopened. A letter itself must strike you as a thing as obsolete as an astrolabe. A letter! Written by hand? In this age—in which we have at our disposal far speedier methods of communication. Nor is my writing particularly artful, as I was born *siniestra*, which, as we all know, has always proved an impediment to graceful penmanship (associations with the satanic notwithstanding).

But I digress. I write once more to request your assistance. I have never been one to dabble in gossip, much less legend, yet I feel a need to share what I consider disturbing events. The first, when I received in the mail a book. A university friend I'd fallen out with over a dispute (when will I learn never to speak of religion or politics?) sent me an anthology of short stories by women writers from South America. Perhaps you take this as less than remarkable, but to break decades of silence with such a gift touched me. Upon opening the book, I read the following inscription dated December 1987: "To K, for all the countess' you have known." Bells went off in my head; my heart pounded. For all of the countesses I have known? As though it was possible to could count countesses on an abacus: one, two, three... ten countesses? Countesses hardly come in multiples; one does not add or divide or multiply noble lineage. Pretenders there will always be, but I recognize one and only one countess—our ancestor, renowned throughout her lifetime, without whom the Kingdom of Hungary would have most certainly gone to the Turks: the lady Erzsébet Bathory,

Tempted I was to toss the book aside, and yet curiosity overcame my better judgment. I turned to the table of contents and there, among such titles as "Latin Lover," "The Guerillero," and "Tigrela," I read: "The Bloody Countess" by Alejandra Pizarnik. "Oh, but it couldn't be," I cried, "not this, not again." Would you believe me

Hummingbird Review

KATHRYN A. KOPPLE

if I told you the book slipped from my hands? And there, lying on the floor before me, I kicked it across the room. In my agitation, I wished to do more than that; I wanted to take a match to the book, burn every page, until nothing would be left but ash, cinders—thus incinerating yet another scandal sheet meant to inflame Erzsébet's reputation.

Centuries come and go: revolution, war, floods and famine. Over three hundred years have passed and still plebian historians write of our lady as the blood countess. She has only "bloody Mary" to keep her company. Mary, Queen of England, was not fit to darn the stockings of our mistress. Erzsébet was no Catholic and for the love of our Lord and Savior made no secret that she was a true and faithful Protestant. How else could she have borne a son, healthy and proud, while Mary had not one child?

I need only to copy here fragments of Pizarnik's story for you to form a full impression, to comprehend the extent of my outrage. "Except for a few baroque refinements—like the Iron Maiden, death by water, or the cage—the Countess restricted herself to the monotonously classic style of torture…" "…several tall girls …after binding their hands, the servants would whip the girls until their bodies ripped and they became a mass of swollen wounds…" "The blood spurted like fountains…" "Nor could the lady remain idle… Sometimes she would lend a hand, and then, impetuously, tear at the flesh—in the most sensitive places." Whatever could the authoress have meant by that! What sensitive places, I ask? Oh, but the lies don't end there. I could go on: maidens scored with hot irons, tiny pincers and knives, blood that soaked the Countesses' white garments through and through. I will spare you the most lurid details. The decadent style has never been to my taste, and even less so when all restraint has been cast aside—replaced instead by a relish for pornography the likes of which haven't their equal in a novel by the Marquis de Sade.

I did take some comfort in the fact that the anthology itself, though possibly well-received in literary circles, would never reach

KATHRYN A. KOPPLE

a wide audience. Many a long night I spent scouring the paper for articles, book reviews—and found no mention of the "blood countess." For that reason, I decided not to write a letter of condemnation to the editor and demand the story censored in the harshest terms; although, we are well within our rights to do so, as it does nothing but distort in the spirit of sadism the memory of our glorious countess Erzsébet.

And then, some twenty years later, another fictionalized tale surfaced—this one published by a writer, who claims ancestral ties to the Countess. The coincidence between the two works is banal enough: again, Erzsébet is described in dust jackets as a vain and cruel woman; one who consorted with witches, spent her days gazing at her reflection in the mirror, all the while cursing the passage of time, her fading youth and beauty, and finally, having lost her senses, bathed herself in the blood of virgins. If only they knew the truth! Our Erzsébet needed no witches, or blood libels. It was her purity that allowed her to retain a perennially youthful appearance. To have been born so unspeakably beautiful is a gift from our Lord God that cannot be undone; not by nature, or time.

Are we who bear the name "Bathory" to continue to allow ourselves abused in this fashion? These accusations will never go away unless we take action. I write to beg you to join me in my cause. I have few resources at my disposal, having never married. I have no children to support me (although, much like our Countess, I have lost none of the vigor of my youth—or my fine looks. Again, I say, we Bathory women are ageless by virtue of our noble ancestry and devotion to the Protestant cause.) I am uncertain as to the extent of the funds necessary to bring a lawsuit. We may be speaking of millions. I fear we are fighting goliaths—as now Hollywood has gotten hold of Erzsébet. "The Countess" has made her way to the silver screen. Ever vigilant, I have watched the movie and though the actress is lovely, this cinematic feat does little to do away with the horrid legend. The ending is revolting. Erzsébet is walled up in her castle, where she dies in the throes of madness, only to be cast

Hummingbird Review

KATHRYN A. KOPPLE

into a potter's grave, scarcely clothed, her limbs splayed in a most grotesque and un-Christian fashion.

My most esteemed cousin, if you cannot find it in yourself to give me the necessary monetary support, could you at least return my letter? I spend my days imagining you in your castle, busy with important affairs of State, and dining at sumptuous tables. I realize you are a man of stature—and I, your American relation, must seem a figment—given that we have never met in person. Alone, my dear relative, I can do little to sponge clean the reputation our beloved Erzsébet.

Remember the authoress I mentioned? Pizarnik? Well, it seems she took her own life; people will one day make something of this—the curse of the blood countess and all. However, I am grateful. May all who disparage the noble lady search their conscience— and should they find it wanting, take similar measures.

Your most devoted servant,
Katalin Bathory Nadasdy

Note: In December 1987, my good friend Julie sent me the anthology *Other Fires: Short Fiction by Latin American Women* (edition Alberto Manguel). She inscribed the title page with the date and words: "Dec. 1987, to Kathy, for all the countess' we have known." At the time, I had recently entered the Ph.D. program at NYU in Latin American literature—and it was because of Julie that I first discovered the fantastic and gruesome legend surrounding the Countess Erzsébet Bathory.

Erzsébet belonged to distant a time and era—the sixteenth century. She was born to a family of Hungarian nobility and married into the powerful Nadasdy family. She bore six children (two died); Katalin Bathory Nadasdy was her third surviving child.

Katalin has disappeared from history but her mother lives on as a serial killer; a woman who allegedly abducted hundreds of young women (all virgins), bled them to death, and bathed in their blood. In 2009, *The Countess*, a film about Bathory directed by Julie Delpy, made its debut. Delpy, who plays Bathory, gives an excellent performance. Romance, political and religious intrigue, and the social position of woman to power are major themes. It is, as expected, a bloody movie, one that becomes painful to watch as Delpy portrays Bathory's descent into madness. Whether Bathory was set-up by her enemies in an effort to seize her property and wealth, or whether she is guilty of the horrendous crimes historians, novelists, and filmmakers attribute to her is something we will never know for certain. After researching Bathory's life, I am inclined to take a sympathetic view of the Countess.

A last word must be said about Alejandra Pizarnik. She is one of Argentina's most esteemed poets. "La condesa sangrienta," while written in prose, demonstrates her lyrical talents to great effect; the story can be found in English in the anthology mentioned above. Her life too offers us a cautionary tale, not all that different from Bathory's. According to biographers, Pizarnik was obsessed with her looks, often taking amphetamines to avoid weight gain. She committed suicide (it may have been a drug overdose) at the age of thirty-six. Bathory was fifty-four when she died, a prisoner in her castle.

ELLEN WADE BEALS

Hey Teacher

I took this class because Exposition 102 was closed and I need an English credit. I saw it was poetry and I thought: how hard can that be? Learn by doing – I guess you could say that has always been my motto, but truth be told, I just thought of it now, realized it is the story of my life – you know, thrown into things – water, sex, motherhood. What does poetry got to do with me anyway? Movies may be about slumdogs, and the word ghetto may describe a fashion trend, but being poor, that's only good when it's Mother Teresa and faraway places. What could be more boring than ordinary poor? Who wants to read about bad paint and stuck windows, the day-old bakery, socks with their toes folded over, and Top Ramen six nights in a row? If I were to send a poem to some magazine, the editor would send it back: –"Sorry – we're not into white trash stories." Poetry is about beautiful women, trees, and death--poems are always about death, almost everything is. But the stylings of a struggling student at a community college? They don't even rap about this shit. Nothing is worse than boring and less than average, less than median, less than anything. I can't even work up a rant. Just give me a C, please.

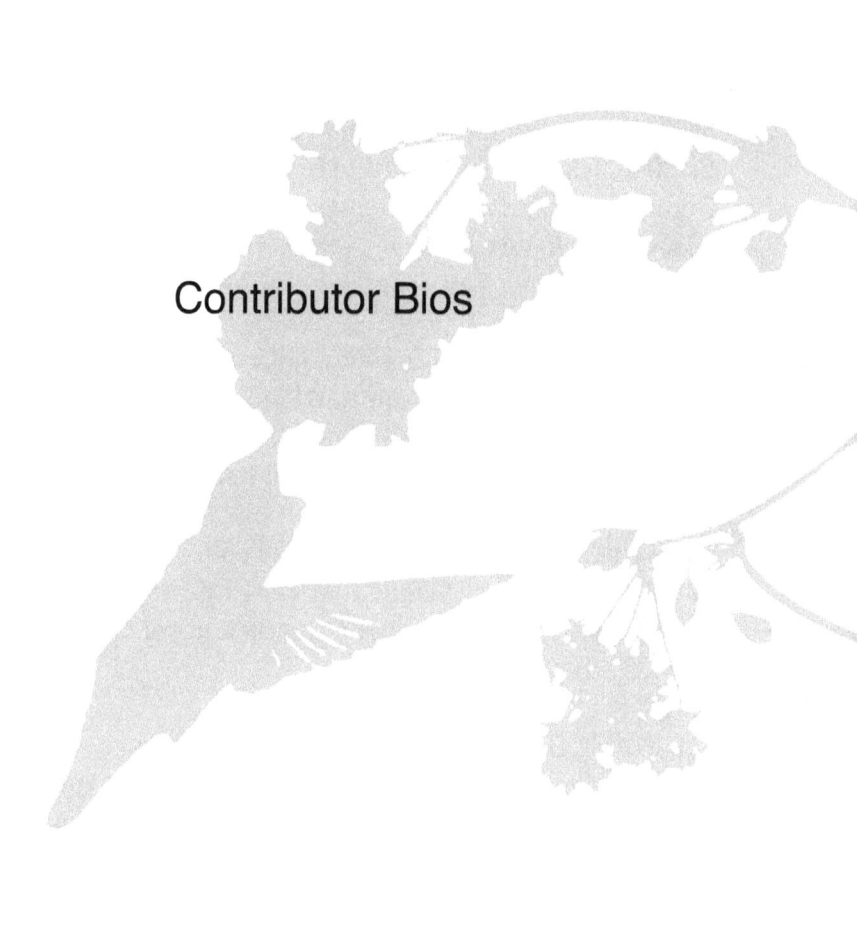

Contributor Bios

CONTRIBUTOR BIOS

RYKA AOKI has an MFA in Creative Writing from Cornell University, where she won a University Award from the Academy of American Poets. A returning contributor to *The Hummingbird Review*, is the author of the chapbook, *Sometimes Too Hot the Eye of Heaven Shines*, from which an excerpt appears in *The Hummingbird Review*; and the forthcoming novel, *He Mele a Hilo*. Two of her compositions were adopted by the American Association of Hiroshima-Nagasaki A-Bomb Survivors as its "Songs of Peace." In 2010, she won the RADAR's Eli Coppola Poetry Chapbook Competition (Incognito Press). Her poems have appeared in the *Jacaranda Review, Asian American Literary Review, Lodestar Quarterly, Grand Street,* and the *Southern Poetry Review.*

ELLEN WADE BEALS (www.solaceinabook.com) writes poetry and prose. Her work has appeared in literary magazines, in anthologies and on the web. In 1999, her short story, "Picking," was awarded *Willow Springs* fiction prize and her poetry has placed in local contests (sponsored by Evanston Library, The Guild Complex, and www.chicagopoetry.com). She is the editor and publisher of *Solace in So Many Words* (Weighed Words LLC, an imprint of Hourglass Books), and she has been working on a novel "for what seems like forever," as she puts it.

MICHAEL BLAKE is the author and screenwriter of the acclaimed novel and motion picture, *Dances With Wolves*. He won the 1991 Academy Award for Best Screenplay. Based in southeastern Arizona, he's also the author of *Airman Mortenson, Marching to Valhallas, The Holy Road, Indian Yell, Twelve the King* and *Into the Stars*, as well as his memoir, *Like a Running Dog*. Michael has been honored with the Environmental Media Award, Golden Quill, American Library Association award and Eleanor Roosevelt award.

GAIL BORNFIELD is an educator, author and poet based in Tucson, AZ. The author of two novels and six educational titles, she was previously published in the Spring, 2011 issue of *The Hummingbird Review*.

JOHN DOE is half of the dynamic singer/songwriter duo for X, a seminal American punk rock and rockabilly band based in Los Angeles, that continues to tour more than 35 years after its formation. He is also an author, actor, poet, and successful solo recording artist with a distinct interest in western lore. He has appeared in more than 30 motion pictures and 20 TV shows and series. The song lyrics in this issue come from his work with X, and also from his 2007 solo release, *A Year in the Wilderness*.

MARTIN ESPADA is a 2007 Pulitzer Prize finalist and author of 13 poetry collections. He has also written three books of essays, most recently *The Lover of a Subversive is Also a Subversive*. Espada is one of the most celebrated poets in the Western Hemisphere, and the recipient of numerous awards and honors including a National Endowment for the Arts Creative Writing Fellowship, Pushcart Prize, Robert Creeley Award, Guggenheim Fellowship, Paterson Award for Sustained Literary Achievement, and 2012 International Latino Book Award. He was a 2007 Pulitzer Prize finalist for his collection, *The Republic of Poetry*. He teaches poetry at the University of Massachusetts.

JOHN GARDINER has published 10 collections of poetry. His literary journal and anthology credits include *Anthology of California Poets, Spillway, Blue Satellite, Speakeasy, Write Bloody, Moon Tide Press, Poetry Flash, Windflower Press* and *The Comstock Journal*. In addition to the United States, he has read in Russia, the Czech Republic, Italy, Germany, Ireland and Brazil. He teaches Shakespeare and poetry for the Gifted Students Academy at University of California-Irvine.

ERICA GOSS won the 2010 Many Mountains Moving Poetry Contest. Her chapbook, *Wild Place*, is forthcoming from Finishing Line Press. Recent work appears in *Hotel Amerika, Rattle, Eclectica, Blood Lotus, Café Review, Connotation Press, Comstock Review,* and *Lake Effect*. She won the first Edwin Markham Poetry Prize, judged by California's Poet Laureate Al Young, and was nominated for a Pushcart Prize in 2010. Erica teaches writing and humanities and is a contributing editor for Cerise Press.

KATE HARDING is a Southern California poet whose work, "The Gourd Song," originally appeared in *Santa Monica Disposal & Salvage*, a collection written under her pseudonym, Penny Perry. She is a Pushcart Prize nominee in both poetry and fiction. Her vast publishing credits include *Redbook, California Quarterly, Poetry International, Earth's Daughters, Compass Rose, Perigee, Limestone Circle, Phoebe* and the *San Diego Poetry Annual*.

JENNIFER HILLMAN is a writer, blogger, poet, radio host and intuitive healer based in Tucson, AZ. She wears many hats and dabbles in as much of life as she can. She describes her writing as "reflective process and inner growth; embracing the passionate nature of myself– a vulnerable, nurturing truth with a strong determination, mixed with the fragility of the feminine." She has been previously published in *The Hummingbird Review*, among other journals.

THEA IBERALL is a poet, novelist and scientist. She has published more than 40 poems in anthologies and journals, including *Rattle, Spillway* and *The Southern California Anthology*. She was a semifinalist in the Atlanta Review International Poetry Competition, and was featured in the documentary *GV6 THE ODYSSEY: Poets, Passion & Poetry*. She is a nationally recognized performance poet, and author of the collection of contextual poems, *The Sanctuary of Artemis*. Now working on her novel, *The Swallow & The Nightingale*, Thea was editor of *The Hummingbird Review*'s Spring 2012 issue.

KATHRYN KOPPLE was Editor of *The Hummingbird Review*'s premier issue. She is a regular contributor of poetry and essays who specializes in Latin American literature. Her translations and essays have appeared in a variety of literary reviews and anthologies, including *These Are Not Sweet Girls, Exact Change Yearbook,* and

The Xul Leader. She has also published original works of poetry in *Contemporary Haibun Online* and *Danse Macabre*. She lives in Philadelphia, PA.

RICKI MANDEVILLE's poems have appeared in *Comstock Review, San Pedro River Review, The Prairie Journal, Spot Lit, 200 New Mexico Poems* and numerous other publications. She is co-founder and consulting editor of Moon Tide Press and has edited more than 18 volumes of poetry. An educator and public speaker, she lives and writes near the ocean in Huntington Beach, CA, and is the author of *A Thin Strand of Lights* (Moon Tide Press) and *Beneath My Bed* (FarStarFire Press).

CLAUDETTE MARCO is a novelist and poet who combines poetic and lyrical structure with a love of fantasy authors and writings. She is working on her novel, *The Sword & The Satchel*, book one of a trilogy, that focuses upon a rarely-featured characterization within the fantasy genre: empowered teenage girls. She lives near Los Angeles.

DAVID MILTON is a writer and artist whose unique application of watercolors and oils achieves a remarkable depth of color and emotional intensity. Milton has re-created with an eye for detail, vintage architecture of the 1930s, 40s and 50s on paper and canvas. His work is held in many corporate collections, including 20th Century Fox Studios in Los Angeles, and Bank of America World Headquarters in San Francisco, along with numerous private collections. His paintings have been exhibited in many museums including the Palm Springs Desert Museum, the Laguna Beach Art Museum, the Winston Churchill Museum, the Taos Art Museum and the Mississippi Museum of Art. He coauthored the screenplay *Bayonets and Blood* with Ret Talbot.

DEAN NELSON is the founder and host of the annual Writer's Symposium by the Sea at Point Loma Nazarene University in San Diego, the program at which Billy Collins appeared in February

2013. Others who have appeared include the late Ray Bradbury, George Plimpton, Kathleen Norris, Joseph Wambaugh, Bill Moyers and many others. The founder and director of the university's journalism program, Dean is the author or co-author of 12 books, most recently *God Hides in Plain Sight: How to Find the Sacred in a Chaotic World*. He is a contributor to *The New York Times, Boston Globe, Christianity Today, Sojourners* and others, as well as receiving multiple Society of Professional Journalists awards.

MANNY PACHECO is an author, journalist and Southern California television and radio personality. He is an Emmy Award nominee, and Best Weblog nominee from the Los Angeles Press Club Southern California Journalism Awards. He's the author of two books, *Forgotten Hollywood Forgotten History,* and *Sons of Forgotten Hollywood Forgotten History*. He also hosts a radio show from which the books arose, "Forgotten Hollywood." He is a member of the Screen Actors Guild and American Federation of Television and Radio Artists.

ROXANNE PILAT is a doctoral candidate in the Program for Writers in the Department of English at the University of Illinois at Chicago. Her work has been published in the *Chicago Tribune,* the *Chicago Sun-Times,* and *Windows* and *Hummingbird Review* literary journals. She is a founding editor of the *Packingtown Review* journal of arts and scholarship.

NEFRETETE RASHEED is an educator, dancer, writer and therapist. Originally from Washington D.C., she has received poetry and theater awards from the New Jersey State Council on the Arts, Princess Grace Foundation, D.C. Arts and Humanities Commission, and the National Academy of American Poets. She was one of several American poets to participate in a reading tour of Russia, sponsored by the Soviet Writers Union. As a Geraldine Dodge Foundation, she wrote, read and conducted writing workshops. Her work has appeared in numerous literary journals.

ADAM RODMAN has written a number of screenplays and teleplays, including his best-known work, *The Serpent and the Rainbow*. Major TV credits include *Fame, CBS Schoolbreak Special, Unforgivable, Rescuers: Stories of Courage: Two Families*, and the "An Old Ghost Walks the Earth" for the *Vietnam War Story* TV series. In 2007, he starred in *Speeders*. A professional writer since his college days, he is currently working on a historical drama, as well as his debut novel.

JOHN ROULEAU carries the distinction of being the only poet to appear in every issue of *The Hummingbird Review*. He was raised on the Saint Croix River in Wisconsin and Minnesota, which informed his love of environment, nature and the simple beauty of place. He also is an artist. John is completing a book of poetry and prose with matched illustrations. He, his wife and daughter live just outside San Francisco.

STEVIE SALAS is the Contemporary Music Advisor to the Smithsonian Institution, and curator of the pop music culture exhibit at the National Museum of the American Indian. He has recorded 10 solo albums noted for both their strong lyrics and musical virtuosity, written the score for the late 1980s hit movie *Bill & Ted's Excellent Adventure*, and embarked on world tours as lead guitarist for Rod Stewart, Mick Jagger, and Terence Trent D'Arby (now Sananda Maitreya). He is working on his memoir, *When We Were the Boys*.

RET TALBOT is an award-winning freelance writer living in midcoast Maine. A graduate of the creative writing programs at Wheaton College (Norton, MA) and the University of St. Andrews (St. Andrews, Scotland), his work has been published in a number of national and international publications. He coauthored the screenplay *Bayonets and Blood* with David Milton.